Dennis has established himself as a true pillar of marketing for the casino industry. His insightful casino knowledge and likeable communication style have forged his ability to passionately educate an entire generation of casino marketers.

—*Troy Simpson, Senior Vice President of Innovation, Barona Valley Ranch Resort & Casino*

Dennis can best be described as *smart* and *sensible*. Smart is a statement of the obvious. What's interesting about this is, he doesn't present himself in a high-brow "cerebral" manner which sometimes leads people to underestimate just how intelligent he is ... but this is always a short-lived perception. What's so telling about Dennis is that he finds this misconception amusing and waits until just the right moment, to come forward with a brilliant solution to what was originally presented as a complex problem. Now "sensible" is not a particularly sexy descriptor, but I define Dennis this way because it has everything to do with his ability to simplify the complex, cut through the clutter and deliver the "simply magnificent" solution. So many people, particularly consultants (I apologize upfront to those in this noble profession), work in reverse. Meaning, they spend time making the problem bigger so that when they come to the conclusion, it's the great "Ah Ha" moment. Dennis doesn't think that way — too much time would be wasted in the process vs. the idea generation. This is the magic of Dennis — that no problem is too big to solve. Creative minds are best stimulated when the problem is simplified and we're all better if we can laugh along the way.

—*Ginny Shanks, CMO, Multimedia Games*

Dennis turned on the light for me to a new way of defining casino marketing. The idea that "marketing is not a department" and using customer service as the foundation of a successful marketing strategy have proven to produce rewards over and over. I have learned that everything that happens is based on our relationships we create. I can now depend on Dennis and the Raving Associates to always to be there to help me with my marketing challenges and celebrations.

—*Michael Peters, Assistant General Manager, Little Creek Resort Casino*

I've been deeply involved with tribal gaming since 1985. As this brand new industry was born — and began growing — there were a number of areas lacking talent and experience. No area was more wanting than casino marketing. Dennis Conrad and Raving Consulting came on the scene with the solution; they shared their vast cumulative casino marketing experience with any and all that asked. When I think of how important Dennis and Raving are to the industry that I love I often think of George Bailey, Jimmy Stewart's character in "It's a Wonderful Life." George was allowed to see how different his home town of Bedford Falls would be if he had never shown up. It wasn't a pretty sight. Well, if Dennis had never shown up to help the Indian gaming industry grow, things would look very different today and frankly wouldn't be nearly as large or profitable.

—*Don Speer, Founder and Chairman, VCAT, LLC*

CONRAD ON CASINO MARKETING

By Dennis Conrad

RAVING CONSULTING COMPANY PRESS
475 Hill Street, Suite G
Reno, Nevada 89501

For information write to Raving Consulting Company
475 Hill Street, Suite G, Reno, Nevada 89501
Telephone (775) 329-7864 Fax (775) 329-4947
E-mail: thebest@ravingconsulting.com

ISBN: 9780615233895

First Printing: 2008

Printed in the U.S.A.

Conrad on Casino Marketing is dedicated to all of the gaming executives that I consider to be "one of us" — the dedicated managers proud to work in the gaming industry — who realize that there is nothing more important than building meaningful relationships with casino customers and employees.

Contents

Foreword

I first met Dennis Conrad in 2001 at the final World Gaming Congress and Expo in Las Vegas. A junior editor with *Casino Journal* at the time, I was patrolling the exhibit floor meeting new people while also trying to get a quote or two on a marketing-related article I was working on. A colleague told me I should go talk to Dennis as he'd be a good source and contact for future marketing questions. So I tracked him down.

My first impressions of Dennis were that he was quirky, talkative ... perhaps a bit *too* energetic about marketing. Yet, even after our very brief five-minute discussion, I came away with more solid information about marketing than I ever could have imagined. I found myself genuinely liking Dennis, but like nearly all journalists, I had a healthy suspicion of ulterior motives and whether our conversation would lead to him "bugging" me constantly for coverage of his still-young Raving Consulting Company.

Yet, it was I who wound up "bugging" him. Several months after the show, I needed some information on yet another article that touched on strong marketing efforts. I picked up the phone and called Dennis at his Reno office. What ensued was a nearly two-hour-long conversation in which he not only helped with my article, but recommended other sources and offered to keep me abreast of marketing-related information that might help me in the future. He became one of my best sources.

Shortly after becoming *Casino Journal's* managing editor, as I was editing Dennis' first column since returning to the magazine after a far-too-long absence, I realized his true *passion* for casino marketing. In this and all of his columns that followed over the next five-plus years, his often simple, no-nonsense advice to bettering casinos' marketing practices jumped off the page at me every time. His columns were real. His tips, musings, anecdotes, praises of good marketing efforts and sharp critiques of bad ones were all solid. He backed up each with real solutions and reader response was genuinely and overwhelmingly positive.

Dennis' writings didn't self-serve or try and overly "sell" his company. He didn't play the game of dangling half-answers to real-world marketing issues. He simply told it how he saw it ... never afraid to give his two cents. When I became *Casino Journal's* editor in late-2005, Dennis was the first person to congratulate me. I, meanwhile, made it a point to increase coverage of a lot of the fun and unique things that Dennis and Raving were doing: his Best and Worst Casino Promotions; the Romero Awards for Excellence in Casino Marketing; Raving's unique, impactful, fun conferences and more.

As I got to know Dennis personally over the past seven or so years, I've seen how his energetic, sometimes kooky, sometimes stern style is not just limited to writing columns or hosting conferences and events. Dennis is a legitimate people person. He takes the time to address every issue he's presented with, every question he's asked, every piece of advice sought. And if he can't provide the answer, he'll many times find someone who will.

Oh sure, Dennis and I have had a couple of minor disagreements over the years — mostly in editing his copy. But the disagreements have come from the strength and conviction of both of our passions. I'm the writer and editor. He's the marketing guru.

Dennis recently told me that I've always been a fair and valued friend of his company, and thanked me for "taking such good care of him" from the gaming trade publication side. While touched, I feel quite the opposite. See, I consider Dennis a true friend and mentor. Without him in my life, I wouldn't know half of what I know today about casino marketing. That's why I jumped at the chance to work for and alongside Dennis and the rest of the talented Raving team. Yes, this editor turned Raver, and the reasons are simple: Dennis' integrity and his company's respect made me *want* to work with him.

If you haven't met or otherwise connected with Dennis yet, you should — whether you're a casino marketing professional or not. In the pages ahead, you'll see what I'm talking about. You may not always agree with Dennis, but his collection of columns will engage you, make you think, make you strive harder.

And for that, I sincerely thank him.

Andy Holtmann
Vice President of Communications
Raving Consulting Company

Introduction

It's a real ego booster to write a book. It's also hard to sit down and write the damn thing. I'd rather be playing golf, shooting craps — heck, even working on an interesting consulting project for a client — rather than grinding out my somewhat organized thoughts on paper.

But I believe I've found a much easier book-writing method. You just write a couple dozen magazine columns over seven or eight years and, when the time comes, organize them, write a dedication and an introduction and *presto*, you've got a book!

At least that's how I've done it twice now, first with "Conrad's Corners" eight years ago and now with this new effort, "Conrad on Casino Marketing" (John Romero assisted me with advice on having the title say what the hell the book is about).

Perhaps you think this book writing method is cheating. I don't care, it's efficient. And most of you haven't read my columns (from *Casino Journal* and *Native American Casino Magazine*) anyway. Besides, it's my best stuff.

My first book, "Conrad's Corners," had two official printings (I don't count the first few hundred copies which I produced with a copier and spiral binding) representing a few thousand books in total.

And so what if 90 percent of the books were given away as gifts? No one ever refused it.

So even if I hope to actually *sell* a higher percentage of "Conrad on Casino Marketing" books, my main goal is to have casino executives (and others) read it, and perhaps think about the casino business just a little differently … in a way that makes our wild and wonderful industry just a little better and a little more focused on casino customers, employees and communities.

And, in a way where, from a marketing perspective, we stop doing the stupid stuff.

Dennis Conrad
Reno, Nevada
August 9, 2008

Industry Observations

I'll take Isle

First of all, it's great to be back writing for a mainstream gaming publication, especially one as prestigious as *Casino Journal*. Readers who remember my "Conrad's Corner" columns from the old *Casino Executive* days, know that I try to be blunt and that I do not shy away from taking the gaming industry to task when it is called for.

Past readers also know that my perspective on gaming starts with the *casino customer*. Not only am I a frequent gaming customer myself, but in my work as a marketing consultant I have found it to be tremendously valuable to start from the customer (and employee) perspective and work back to the gaming organization itself, to offer meaningful advice and assistance.

That's right. You start from the gaming customer and work back. And that right there summarizes my main issues for the last 30 years with this wonderful business we call "gaming" (I still call it "gambling" but then again I'm not politically correct). In all of our budgets and strategic plans and regulations and staffing ratios and human resources policies — all of that "stuff" — we often forget the *customer* and how he or she experiences what we offer.

As this will be a monthly "marketing" column, it is important to share my definition of what "marketing" is. I like to use the definition in Webster's: "All business activity involved in the moving of goods from the producer to the consumer, including advertising, packaging, selling, etc." This definition speaks to the concept that marketing is not a department, but should be an integrated approach involving all aspects of our casino organizations.

So it's not just about direct mail and research and casino promotions and VIP events and players clubs. It's also about cleanliness and being "easy to do business with" and quick hopper fills and short lines at the cage and knowledgeable employees. *It's about anything that matters to your customers.*

So this column will be a blend of stories and principles and (sometimes) admonishments about listening to our customers and aligning our gaming organizations around the only marketing strategy that I know: Find out what your customers want. Give it to them.

And that's why I like Isle of Capri Casinos. It knows what its customers want and it tries to give it to them.

Isle of Capri could fairly be called a "sleeper" company in the gaming industry. Its properties are not the flashiest, although they are bright and colorful (the Isle parrot is hauntingly effective). Isle properties are not located in Las Vegas or Atlantic City but in places like Boonville, Mo. and Lula, Miss. and Marquette, Iowa.

Isle has been very effective in establishing a "brand," an image that stands out in the minds of its customers. This Caribbean themed brand stands for fun and liveliness and people. And this brand is carried out at all Isle of Capri casinos (with the exception of Isle's Rhythm City property in Iowa), in the design, in the décor, in the collateral, in the uniforms. You *know* when you are in an Isle of Capri property. It's called Isle Style and it's not just an image or a concept but it refers to the very nature of "how we do business around here."

That's not to say that Isle of Capri's success is built on some fuzzy feeling of fun. Isle has been a savvy acquirer of casino properties, hunting in smaller markets that are typically under the radar screen of the Big Four casino companies. It conducts effective, continuing research on its casino customers. It has executed revenue-driving, branded casino promotions. Its IsleOne Players Club is one of the better, more generous players clubs in the country and its IsleMiles component of IsleOne is a unique, value-adding innovation (and appears to have been emulated in Harrah's revamped Total Rewards program). And Isle's focused, scientific, direct mail efforts would rival Harrah's in the database marketing arena.

But what sets Isle of Capri Casinos apart from most other gaming companies is its focus on its employees. Isle Style also refers to the internal branding and communications program where employees are hired with an eye toward "service above self" and subsequent training is recurrent, relevant and, oh my gosh, even *fun* (you should hear the Isle training song "A Complaint Is a Gift"). Isle managers are required to have development plans for their employees and they utilize training and educational programs both inside and outside the gaming industry. I personally witnessed Isle's home grown "Marketing Boot Camp" for its junior marketing executives and have seen nothing like it in the gaming industry.

As most Isle of Capri properties are located in conservative Southern and Midwest gaming jurisdictions, "Isle Style" also has a strong community component to it, building a strong third leg to the customer-employee-community (what else is there?) marketing tripod. Isle is very active in its local host communities. It has made a strong stand on the problem gambling issue. Like Harrah's, Isle employees are very active in volunteering for locally based charities and their cash donations support numerous worthy causes.

Isle of Capri understands that marketing is an integrated process. But more important than that, it understands that the casino business is, or should be, about people. Like Harrah's, it understands that we sell an entertainment experience that enriches people's lives. And while certainly having fun slot games and quality restaurants and desirable retail items can help enrich people's lives, ultimately it is *people* who enrich the lives of *people*.

Isle of Capri understands that. As does Harrah's. As do (too few) other gaming companies.

I never met Bernie Goldstein, the founder of Isle of Capri Casinos, Inc. I do know his story — successful businessman, used his expertise in an unrelated industry to pursue a gaming opportunity in Iowa. I'd hazard a guess that Bernie "gets it." Isle of Capri is a people focused company that should make us all proud to be in the gaming biz. Ya done good, Bernie, ya done good.

17 ways to help your gaming business

Working with a variety of casino clients is interesting, but what is *really* interesting is being a customer of a few hundred casinos and getting a firsthand look at how they do business — their rules, their policies, how their employees act, how they market themselves on their own casino floors. And after seeing all this and talking with literally thousands of casino customers and employees (both formally and informally), I've noticed numerous ways that you can improve the operation of your casino. Some tips are directly related to increased casino revenue. Others will make your customers or employees happier (which should lead to improved revenues!).

So here they are, in no particular order, 17 ways to help your gaming business. It's OK if you don't agree with me, but don't shoot the messenger.

17 ways to help your gaming business:

1. ***Make four 10-hour shifts common in your organization*** — Employees love this 40-hour work week. They get an extra day off and have a better attitude. It can help you get more "hands on deck" on weekends and save on FTEs. So why aren't you allowing "Four Tens?"

2. ***Eliminate all cage lines*** — Look, I don't know how to do this (Hint: your cage cashiers *do*) but it is one of your casino customers' biggest peeves. Hire more cashiers, have your supervisors work a window, heck, drop a few ineffective billboards and start your Cage Service Marketing Program!

3. ***Require all of your managers to work one day a quarter in a frontline position*** — Oh, they'll hate it at first and whine about being too busy, but what a great way to stay piped in to your business, pinpoint organizational snafus, reward top frontline employees and send the right message about your casino!

4. ***Turn your craps dealers into marketers*** — The most fun table game should have the best employee interactions. So get those

craps croupiers joking (with customers, not each other), teaching, entertaining, inviting in players to play and making a "great time, every time" (to steal an old Harrah's phrase).

5. ***Get more penny and nickel slots*** — Or did you not notice that these games get more play, have a higher hold percentage and get results comparable to 25 cents and $1 slot machines?

6. ***Increase the number of winners in your casino promotions and tournaments*** — Sure a life-changing prize has some value, but I believe common sense dictates that it is better to give 10,000 casino players $100 each than to give one lucky player $1 million. I'm betting that somehow those $100 bills all work their way back to your casino vault.

7. ***Insist that your senior executives eat lunch only in the employee dining room*** — Hey, I like being waited on in the coffee shop or specialty restaurant as much as the next guy does, but think about the message you send to your employees by breaking bread with them (and make sure the honchos do indeed dine with them, and not create some elite "executive table" amidst the troops).

8. ***Get ticket-in/ticket-out, "pouch pay," machine fill bags under machines*** — and any other device, process, product, innovation, or procedure that improves the speed and efficiency of your slot service. This is the heart of your business and the one area where *no one* — not you, not your customers, not your employees — wants slow slot service. So do something about it.

9. ***Quit funneling every living being through your players club booth*** — You know what I mean: bus customers, coupon clippers, entertainment ticket buyers, retail purchasers, jackpot redeemers, information seekers, etc. This is the area for starting and nurturing relationships with your better customers, not destroying them.

10. ***Have more signs of "Welcome" at your entryways*** — and less signs stressing "Rules of Prohibited Conduct" and how you can kick me out for any reason you wish.

11. ***Stop making your customers endure multiple lines for a single transaction*** — What, you don't know what I mean? Well, I'm kind of thinking of those situations where you get your coupon for a free roll of nickels at the welcome center, you get your players club card and a printed voucher for your roll of nickels at the club and your actual roll of nickels at the cage (with a three part form to be given to security … just kidding).

12. ***Attack restaurant lines*** — I don't know what will work here for you, whether it's an overhead paging system, beepers, better staffing, *whatever*. But I do know that while they are standing in your food lines, they ain't gambling.

13. ***Train every employee to sell*** — I realize this will take some effort and expense, but think what will happen when your valet parker recommends your buffet, your security officer mentions the video poker progressive jackpot near the entrance and your blackjack dealer tells his players how they can buy the cool logo shirt he's wearing.

14. ***Stop the "No Mid-Shoe Entry" rule at your casino's blackjack games*** — I know why you think you need it, but you are frustrating players trying to get in the game and costing yourself hundreds of thousands of extra blackjack hands per year. Train your floor people and surveillance people better and stop shooting yourself in the foot.

15. ***Send a welcome letter (and offer to return) to every new players club member*** — and do it within one week of when they joined!

16. ***Quit having your entertainment events on weekends*** — I know you like the buzz Willie Nelson creates on Saturday night in your

showroom, but he also drives away your best slot players (who can't get on *their* machine) and clogs your parking lot, restaurants and other services. Book Willie when you need the biz.

17. ***Quit paying lip service to your non-smoking gaming area*** — It's one of the biggest complaints that I hear from customers ("too smoky") and two-thirds of the adult universe doesn't smoke (what an opportunity!). So stop putting your non-smokers in that cramped area, with the poor selection of games, where no one wants to play!

In fact, if you stop doing everything that your customers don't like, you won't need my 17-item list at all. You'll need just one good ear.

There is superstition

Gamblers are superstitious; there is no doubt about it. In my 30 years of working in and frequenting casinos, I have seen a number of superstitions in those "crazy gamblers." In fact, even though I understand all of the math and the casino inner workings, I struggle myself with those insidious superstitious urges.

I know you've heard them:

- "When the dice leave the table, the next roll will be a seven" (this will actually happen once every six times).

- "I never win with my players club card in the slot machine" (the card being in the machine will not affect the results of that game).

- "I like to play on Mondays after the weekend crowd has loaded up the hoppers" (random number generation makes this impossible).

- "A bad player on third base affects the whole blackjack game for the worse" (whether a player is bad or good does not affect the math of blackjack or your chances of winning).

- "Old slot machines pay better than new slot machines" (maybe, maybe not, it all depends how you set the theoretical hold percentage of the game).

You get the picture. Most casino players are superstitious in one way or another. In fact, most operators doubt that casinos could stay in business if they weren't. They reason that, if these players *really* understood that we offer (mostly) negative expectation games where our customers are guaranteed to lose over time, do you think they would continue to give us their money???

This existing culture of customer superstition raises some interesting marketing issues and probably some moral issues as well. I mean, if customers think Megabucks is due to hit because the progressive jackpot on it is high, do you pander to that superstition and run a Megabucks promotion? Do you announce all of your jackpot winners on your overhead P.A. system so people will (superstitiously) think, "everyone is winning around here?"

I remember several years ago when a slot manufacturer developed a "near miss" machine that had a normal hold percentage, but had numerous reel combination results that suggested that a jackpot had "just missed" (you know, first reel stops on "seven" very often, second reel stops on "seven" and the third reel is a "Bar" — a tantalizingly "close" loser). The Gaming Control Board vetoed the notion of this "near miss" game (thankfully), saying it was a deceptive industry practice.

So how do we deal with our customers' superstitions in our casino marketing and our business practices? My answer might surprise you, and it was shaped by my early casino career experience where I was a table game instructor who had six lessons a day, teaching wide-eyed, potential new customers how to play the various table games.

My "job" was experimental in nature and since there was no job description, I had to create my own instructional style. Since I was myself a savvy gambler wannabe, I soon began giving my customer-students the straight scoop on the various bets and steering them to the most mathematically advantageous wagers. Yes, my table games manager reprimanded me for "wising them up." But I continued my down and dirty instruction, albeit a little more discreetly. And here's what I discovered.

When you give your customers honest information on your games (and I mean it has to be *absolutely* honest), a few things happen:

1. They become more confident — feeling less like suckers — and will be more likely to try a new game and play it longer.

2. No matter how hard you try to strip away their shroud of superstitions with facts, they still cling to their superstitions.

3. They are thankful for the information (even if they may not completely "get it") and the opportunity to more fully enjoy their gaming experience.

Now to me, this seems like a pretty powerful marketing result — thankful, more confident gamers ready to spend their money with you. But as an industry, our approach to this concept, regrettably, is to keep our customers "fat, dumb and happy" and earn a (suspected) higher rate of return from these casino goers while they learn the ropes.

In my opinion, this is shortsighted and just gives gaming industry opponents more ammunition to accuse us of being predatory. It also provides some impetus to regulators to require gaming companies to do things like printing the odds of winning on the back of lottery tickets, insisting on minimum payback percentages on slot machines, or even worse (now in Canada and Australia), limiting how long slot players can play and what denomination of currency they can insert in the bill validator.

If I am right about this concept of full disclosure to our customers, then it makes sense to list all of the theoretical hold percentages on our slot machines, to offer blackjack instruction to our guests that includes how to play "basic strategy," and listing how often you can theoretically expect to hit all six numbers on your six-spot keno ticket. In fact, disclosing these deep, dark, mathematical casino secrets will not only allow you to promote your "loose" slot machines, but will also offer the opportunity to honestly trumpet exactly "how loose" they are.

And what I suggest will happen is that your honesty in marketing will build more trust with your customers, more respect with your employees and more latitude with your regulators and your communities. And this in turn will have a positive business result for your gaming operation.

But I am not naïve. I know this notion will be received by most gaming operators about as warmly as a visit from the in-laws. But I would like to encourage you to imagine a world where we are so proud and confident of our product that we are willing, even eager, to tell our customers all about it. A world where our customers are truly our guests and our friends ... not some suckers to be plundered. A world where we strip the last remaining veil of secrecy from our business, because ultimately all it does is throw up another barrier to building meaningful customer relationships.

How to have a great player development function

I have done a lot of work with a lot of different casinos around the process of "player development," which despite its sinister name with its laboratory rat connotations, does serve an extremely valuable purpose, namely the identification, retention and increased spending of casino players. Most casinos have some sort of players club and/or host department built to support its player development function.

What I have discovered across Casino Land regarding player development has been pretty shocking. Whether it's large or small casinos, traditional or Native American operations, older or newer marketing functions — very little strategic thinking has gone into player development and consequently the majority of efforts I've seen are unorganized, inadequate, often immeasurable, highly compartmentalized and missing significant opportunities. Some casinos pay lip service to player development. Others have created ethically-suspect, high-pressure sales operations that would make some arm-twisting car dealerships proud.

My main concerns around the current state of casino player development center around a few key things. First, it is usually treated as an isolated function done by a few people in a single department, rather than an integrated process involving many employees and departments that touch customers. Often, those player development employees are outsiders hired with purloined customer lists.

Second, current player development efforts focus mainly on "hand holding" with current VIP customers and not enough on focused energy against finding new players. Other current shortcomings include lack of effective measurement of player development programs, little regard for problem gambling issues with developed players and little use of current customers and employees to help drive business from their own personal networks. All in all, not a very pretty picture for the chief business development function for most casinos.

So what are we to do? How can we build great player development into our casino operations? Unfortunately, current state-of-the-art-examples are few and far between. Barona Valley Ranch is probably as good as it gets right now, with its focus on player development and its progressive use of Mariposa's CRM software. Most others, including marketing leader Harrah's, grapple with the concept and organizational structure around developing players.

As one who has been wrestling with this issue for many years, allow me to share my thoughts on the key principles I believe are important in having effective, measurable, value adding player development at your casino, large or small:

1. ***Utilize the best people in your organization, create a career path for them in player development and pay them accordingly for the value they bring.*** Using "hired guns" with customer lists for your player development gets you expensive, disloyal executives interested in creating value for themselves — and lists for sale to the competition.

2. ***Have lots of player development personnel and train them relentlessly in sales techniques.*** Whether they are hosts, greeters, slots hosts, marketing executives, players club reps or whatever, you can't have too many "relationship builders" if you are doing it right. Worried about spiraling salaries? Cut the advertising budget in half — this is much more important.

3. ***Work player development into the roles of all your frontline employees who touch customers.*** Food servers, cocktail servers, hotel desk clerks, dealers, slot personnel, casino porters — these are all employees who have opportunities to sell the casino (especially the players club), so get them selling!

4. ***Focus equally on relationship building and relationship maintenance.*** It is human nature for hosts and other player developers to hang out with existing VIPs. Get them spending at least half their time turning strangers into friends.

5. ***Find appropriate measurements for player development success and use them!*** New sign ups, carded headcount percentages, play increases (or decreases) from established players, tracked play of VIPs — these and other scorecards need to be implemented, watched closely and used to make business decisions.

6. ***Pay for performance.*** *Anyone* who can build business for your casino is very valuable to your operation and should be paid for

it, no matter their role. So find ways to reward those employees generating players club signups, getting VIPs to return or keeping players at playing stations!

7. ***Leverage your customers and employees to build new gaming business.*** *Every* customer and employee should have the ability to comp a new player to a buffet or a hotel stay. OK, OK, you have some controls, insist on players club membership as a pre-condition of the comp, and you make future offers based on play. But if the people who work and play with you can't develop business for you, who can?

Player development should not be a mystery, nor should it be something you do because everyone else does. It should be about organized relationship building with company-wide, trained relationship builders who understand what's important to your casino business, and then are encouraged, empowered and rewarded for making it happen.

Things that go bump in the night

Casinos are fun places to be and can often be fun places to work. They certainly are unique environments. For instance, you don't see many keno writers or slot techs out in the "real world."

I truly believe that casinos try hard to be efficient and would like to think that they have a reasonable focus on the customer. Yet something continues to nag at me. As someone who has had tens of thousands of interactions in casinos over the years, who has signed up for hundreds of players clubs, eaten more casino buffets than I care to admit and essentially navigated the rules, procedures and systems in casinos all over the world, I feel it is time to share the casino foibles, disconnects, snarls, impediments and customer unfriendly "goo" that I have witnessed over the last 30 years. Disagree if you will, but if you can address the issues underlying the observations I am about to make, you will become more customer focused, easier to do business with and hopefully a casino that "gets it."

Enjoy my observations from the casino trenches:

- Casino craps departments are very good at clocking every dollar that goes into the drop box and very poor about welcoming a new player into the game.

- Service levels in casinos are best in typical hospitality areas (hotel, restaurant, etc.) and worst in the biggest revenue generating department of all — slots.

- Most casino dealers will take a highlighter pen to your currency before they will acknowledge you.

- Keno is a rip-off, it's always been a rip-off, and then we wonder why no one plays it.

- Although I haven't seen it, it must be possible to *start* with the customer experience and then build rules, procedures, systems and internal controls around it, instead of vice versa.

- The players club staff deals with our best customers and is the closest thing we have to a sales position in a casino. Yet they are usually the lowest paid in the organization and looking to get out of that job as soon as possible. Hello?

- We still scold and jerk around our craps players way too much.

- Although it has gotten slightly better, casino executives spend way too little time with living, breathing customers and not much time on the casino floor on the busiest day — Saturday.

- Except for Harrah's, having an effective, business-building, value-adding Web site is a concept that still eludes most casinos.

- Casinos still spend way too much on advertising, or at least on *bad* advertising.

- Too few casinos study or heed John Romero.

- Yes, poker is hot right now, but just adding or expanding a poker room is not a very strong poker strategy.

- Slot floors across North America have way too few penny machines and way too many dollar machines. Many slot directors still can't see past the word "penny."

- Security officers man most entrances at casinos across North America. Unfortunately, most security officers act like security officers (instead of welcoming hosts) at casinos across North America.

- I don't care what your table games VP tells you; the "No Mid Shoe Entry" rule at your blackjack tables is costing you a lot of money.

- Casino cages and valet parking are two areas in casinos that should have great service, but typically don't.

- Not many casinos talk to, much less listen to, their best customers.

- I still can't believe all the long restaurant lines at casinos, with all the empty tables in the room.

- OK, this is a pet peeve, but there is a growing legion of craps players across North America who "set the dice" when they shoot them (and slow up the game). Can't you at least have the dice stickman deliver the dice preset to these players?

- Non-smoking areas are still nothing more than gestures in most casinos.

- I can't believe the thickness of the walls that still exist between slot and table game departments.

- The biggest missed marketing opportunity in casinos? The highly frequent "regulars" and their $20-, $40- and $100-daily spends.

- If you want to grow your business and have happier customers at your casino, have *great* coffee available everywhere.

- If you could have your employees be good, smooth salespeople, you would *propel* your gaming revenues.

- Although it has gotten better, we don't do enough for our slot winners and we rarely even think about our slot losers.

- The casino environment is still pretty much a maze and a hodgepodge. When we can truly integrate and stage the various lights, sounds and temperatures, we'll really be on to something.

- You want to learn about marketing? Go spend a few days in (most) casinos struggling for survival.

- I never thought I'd say this, but I can see hope for Reno.

- Most players clubs don't contain enough value for players. Don't believe me? Ask your players.

- Repeating myself: the difference between a good casino executive and a great casino executive is about 10,000 customer interactions.

- There is tremendous opportunity to use casino golf courses as player development arms of the casino, if only we can realize what business we are really in.

- Want to know the biggest service and marketing challenge in casinos? Recognizing the opportunity with strangers in your casino.

- I still think retail kiosks would work well in table game pits, where customers could buy *authentic* dice, cards, felts, chips, even dealer shirts and aprons.

- Mr. and Ms. Slot Director? What have you done to promote your new slot games recently? I mean, why wouldn't you want your top 1,000 customers to play every new game first, in test mode, to expose them to your new cash registers?

- This is the last time I'm going to tell you: spend your marketing dollars on the customers who spend their gambling dollars with *you*.

- You'll know you have it when your dealers spend as much time practicing their customer interactions as their shuffling of cards and cutting of chips.

Business cards and other selling tactics

The gaming experience almost sells itself. I mean between the "zings and stings" of the gambling experience, the quality and value of the food, the often headliner entertainment and the myriad of other attractions in the modern day casino, it almost is "Build it and they will come" (except in highly-competitive gaming markets, of course).

Perhaps it is precisely because of the powerful lure of the 21st century casino, that, as an industry, we don't do a very good job of "selling our casinos," of doing the soft selling, the up-selling, the cross-selling, heck *any* selling at all, that will ensure that our guests maximize their spend at our casino hotels and fully enjoy the widest range of our resort experience.

Before you accuse me of being short sighted or too negative on this lack of casino salesmanship, let me say that I have had thousands of employee interactions in hundreds of casinos across North America in my career and I have rarely — or in some cases *never* — witnessed the following from these supposedly trained casino employees:

- A valet parker suggesting that I try the buffet;

- A room reservationist suggesting I upgrade to a mini-suite;

- A blackjack dealer on a dead game asking me to sit down and play; or

- A slot employee, seeing a continued run of bad luck, suggesting I try another game somewhere else in the casino.

In truth, when asked, "Where is a good place to get a steak?" most casino employees are as likely to recommend a place outside the casino (sometimes at a competitor's place!) as anywhere in one of your casino restaurants. Most dealers on a dead game are apt to warn you that they are "hot" and imply that you are taking a grave risk to start up their table, as they are to be warm and welcoming to a sole wandering player. And if you ask any employee to give you details about the $100,000 Cash Giveaway, you're more apt to receive a fairly bland, "Check at the players club" (which is better than the second most common response, "I don't know") than to be fully informed and complimented on participating in such a great casino promotion.

My goal in this column is not to throw stones, but to convince you that turning all of your employees into salespeople is one of the strongest marketing pushes you can undertake, and that our industry does have some good examples of selling tools and protocols that are being used successfully right now. And, as gaming markets continue to mature and growth becomes more dependent on maximizing spend of *customers you already have*, this "selling imperative" will become more and more important.

So to convince you of the need for selling your casino, let me paint two pictures. Both are pictures of the same new customer, each time intending to spend $100 playing your slots for two hours ... longer if their money lasts. In the first example, the customer valet parks, wanders the casino floor, may or may not eat in a restaurant and plays slots for two hours. In the second example (with the same customer), the valet parker recommends that she try the buffet because "it's Italian night and the chef — who is Italian — makes a killer veal parmesan." The greeter at the door asks if the guest has a players club card and is entered in the $100,000 Cash Giveaway. The slot attendant notices the guest is only 20 points short of her first $5 in cash-back and informs her that another five minutes of play will do the trick as well as earn her two more drawing tickets for the $100,000 Cash Giveaway. And a dealer on a dead game, as our guest wanders by, invites her to play blackjack with him and even offers to teach her how to play.

Now which scenario do you think will get the guest to stay longest, spend the most, leave the happiest, come back the quickest and tell the most others about your casino? I knew you'd see the simple and powerful truth of selling your casino experience!!!

And yes there are some great examples of salesmanship in our casinos, if only we'd look and pay heed:

- The Mirage in Las Vegas has had contests and paid bonuses to room reservationists to get booking guests to upgrade to suites.

- Harrah's Rincon reservationists will tell you all about the features and attractions at their property, if you are staying there for the first time.

- Anwar Masud, the general manager at the Siena in Reno works the property's "swipe and win" kiosk line, assisting guests, showing them how to redeem their promotion prize and thanking them for being at the Siena.

- Caesars Palace in Las Vegas has an internal performance standard that says every guest staying at the property for three days, should receive no less than six different managers' business cards.

And speaking of business cards, is there any simple and better way to sell your casino??? Check out these winning examples from our industry:

- Richard Darder, the CEO of Casino Pauma near San Diego has a business card that says, "Casino Pauma is a great place to work and play" and has "Slots, Blackjack, Friendly Staff and Great Food and Drinks."

- Executives at the Pioneer Hotel and Gambling Hall have their property's mission statement on the back of their business cards.

- When Mark Grainger, a gaming supply sales executive, was between jobs, his business card didn't say "Consultant," but rather that he was head of "Job Huntin' Inc." and that he was a "Relocatable, self-motivated, team oriented sales manager."

- Harrah's Las Vegas craps dealers have had business cards stating that they are, "Craps Entertainers with 6 Shows Daily!" and that the room reservation number at Harrah's is 800-Harrahs.

- Dean DiLullo, former GM of Station Casino's Wild Wild West Gambling Hall and Hotel, had an actual "gaming chip business card" that was good for a free drink on a future visit and listed the hotel reservation phone number.

- And finally, Dave Matheson, CEO at Coeur d'Alene Casino in Idaho has a business card that uses the backside to offer a free stay in CDA's new hotel.

These examples prove that yes, you can "sell your casino experience." In fact, very soon, if you want to grow your casino revenues and truly maximize your marketing dollars, it will no longer be an option. It will be a requirement. Might as well get cranking now.

Sometimes a great (service) notion

One of the interesting things that I get to do as a marketing consultant is to talk with a number of casino customers at a wide variety of casinos across North America. I always try to talk with a cross section of a casino's *best* customers, because with the 20/80 rule so firmly in effect at most casinos, the opinions of those VIPs count more than others. If you can make them happy, you're on your way to being a customer-focused casino and are also apt to be "player friendly" for many others who value what they do in a casino experience.

Most of these high-value casino customers are what I would call "regulars" and their opinions are remarkably consistent across many different gaming markets. Essentially these VIPs say "loosen the machines" (especially loosen the machines), "don't take us for granted," and, "fix all of those service staffing and environmental (too hot, too cold, too smoky, too noisy) glitches," and you'll own their business for a long time.

What has always surprised me, however, is the near unanimity of opinion that these VIPs have on the level of customer service. Oh, they can rattle off the names of the lousy employees, but mostly they rate their casino service an eight or a nine on a 10 scale, with many giving it an unqualified "10." What is interesting however, is that these scores are almost *always* higher than what front-line employees and managers rate their own customer service, what service shoppers tend to find and what I myself usually see in my own investigations.

We are giving our best customers pretty good service!

Now don't get me wrong — it is not *great service* (yet) and certainly one would hope that, as much as these high worth regulars spend, it *better be* quality service that they are receiving from our casino staffs. But rather than give the casino industry a giant collective pat on the back, I would rather focus on why most of us get pretty mediocre service from these same casinos that dote on their VIPs. I mean, we *might* be high rollers, too!

First of all, it is natural for employees to be shy or less welcoming to a stranger. It is a human trait and it explains why so few people enjoy door-to-door sales, or why most men have trouble meeting women and why the fear of public speaking (in front of strangers) is more disabling to most people than the fear of snakes.

Second, most regular casino customers tend to be known tippers of known tipping worth. Hey, they've been around the casino scene for years and they know that most front-line casino employees are extremely hard working, as well as extremely dependent on gratuities to earn a decent living. New casino goers or infrequent customers tend to be "less hip" to the "toke" and until they show casino employees some cold, hard appreciation, the employee tendency will be to treat them as the strangers that they are.

Finally, and shame on us, we have not trained our employees well on the real value of building new customer relationships and how to go about that task. Oh sure, many of us now have at least some sort of "customer service training" where we take two hours telling our employees to "be nice." But rarely do you see a comprehensive effort made in educating employees on whom to be nice to, how to be nice and the value of being nice to casino customers.

Obviously, our casino employees' best qualities come out when dealing with our best customers. But how can we have these same qualities come out when strangers are wandering all over our casino floors? After all, our marketing departments spend millions of dollars to get these strangers to come try us. Shouldn't we be at least investing some effort in showing our employees that these "regulars in waiting" are the real keys to growing our casino business? Sure we should!

But no one said that this would be easy. We have to overcome natural tendencies. We have to ask our employees to forego a few tipping opportunities to focus on a few more relationship building opportunities. We have to teach ice-breaking skills. We have to train our employees that when a guest answers affirmatively to the question, "Is it your first time here?" that it should set off a string of responses and a wave of welcoming that are as good as they can muster.

We are all looking for competitive advantages in our casino businesses. Often it is in the quality of our products or the range of our casino resort service. Sometimes it is in our convenient location. Occasionally it is in our players club benefits or the appropriate richness of our direct mail benefits. But rarely have I seen a casino property establish competitive advantage by how it treats its customers, especially strangers.

So the next time you are scouring through budgets or trying to muster approval for capital expenditures, or figuring out how you can get your hands around spiraling costs, stop for a second and think about the thousands of casino customers who are streaming through your doors each week — the strangers — and whether or not they are remaining strangers after one or two visits to your casino property.

If you can turn strangers into friends at your casino or in your business, not only will you have tapped into the simplest form of customer relationship management, but you will be efficiently following up with the thousands of customers that your millions of dollars in marketing has delivered to your doorstep. Sounds pretty smart to me.

The opportunity with the game of craps

One of the best learning things that I do as a consultant is to gamble in casinos across the country. It always amazes me how few casino executives gamble. I can tell you there is no better way to learn about a casino's culture, service, marketing and organization than to actually sit down and play as a gaming customer. I learn more as a frontline customer than I do reading reports or talking with casino managers. I encourage you to (responsibly, of course) gamble. Can't afford it? Give up the social club membership or eat out one day less a month. Hey, gambling is your business!

Anyway, my game of choice is craps. I love the fast-paced nature of the game and the camaraderie at the table. Plus it's a good gamble. My early career experience as a craps dealer probably also accounts for the game's appeal to me.

I realize that not all tribal casinos have the game of craps, depending on tribal compacts and business volumes (you might look into "California Craps" at Casino Pauma near Escondido, Calif. if you want to see a variation of craps that might pass compact muster). I also realize that craps is a difficult game to learn, it is hard to find qualified dealers for it, it is labor intensive and surveillance departments often are challenged in watching it.

I don't care. In my opinion, craps is the single biggest table games revenue opportunity out there for tribal casinos that can have it. While table game operators continue to look at a never-ending parade of new (and usually unsuccessful) table games, craps is sitting right under the noses of most of them.

Let me make my case. Craps is easily the most fun casino table game. Don't believe me? Go spend five minutes at a "hot" dice table. Craps is always the one game that most casino goers secretly wished they knew how to play. I know — I've had hundreds of them tell me so. Craps also has an unparalleled allure. It requires dice. It's the only game where you stand at the table instead of sit. It has its own lingo. It has scores of different bets, with all happening simultaneously. It has the "do" bet and the "don't" bet, whereby the optimists and pessimists at a table can engage in some spirited rivalry.

So why hasn't craps just really taken off? Why has its growth been stagnant and not more people found the joy that I find in the game? Sure, the game is complicated, but the real reason is that *casinos have done a poor job selling craps.* Most casinos do not have craps lessons available. The "gaming guides" for craps are bland, trite and confusing. Craps dealers and floor persons are not given any special training to make the game more fun and user friendly. In fact, at the dice table, rules and regulations hold sway over fun. You'll hear players get scolded for not having the dice reach the end of the table or for rubbing the dice with two hands. You'll hear admonitions about betting early, about keeping one's hands off the layout, about gently setting money down instead of tossing it, about keeping drinks "behind the rail." You'll see craps box persons worry more about logging how much cash has been put in the drop box (won't we know that during soft count anyway?) than about whether or not guests are having a great time.

No wonder potential players are too intimidated to try craps!

So what's the answer? How can you make craps a revenue driving force for your Indian casino? Well there's not a single magic bullet, but the answer, I believe, lies in a whole series of steps that are easy to define, but difficult to execute.

First, I would hire the friendliest, most service-oriented, entertaining dealers I could find in a 100-mile radius from my casino (I don't care if they were experienced or not, you can teach that). Then I would train them and train them some more. I would teach them how to "sell" the game. I would show them how to continually teach new players how to play, as they were dealing the game. I would let them know that one cross word to a craps customer would be ground for termination.

And then when they were certified as premier craps "entertainers" I would double their salary and let them keep their own tips (you probably agreed with me until here). From there, the rest is easy: you promote the game like crazy, you simplify the confusing craps layout, you improve the payouts on some of those usurious "sucker bets," you throw in some fun promotional elements (how about letting dice shooters keep the dice as a souvenir after they've made six or more passes?!).

If you can do all this at your Indian casino (and no, it isn't easy, but it beats watching the game of craps slowly die), I don't see why you can't double your craps revenue next year ... and the year after. For the most fun casino game should certainly be the fastest growing!

Indian Gaming

What Indian gaming customers tell me

I have had the pleasure of doing marketing consulting for three years now and have worked with several dozen Indian casinos. Large destination type facilities … moderately-sized operations … small casinos in remote locations with a few hundred slots and not far removed from their bingo hall roots. Yes, it has been quite a learning experience.

In this time, I have had the occasion, both formally and informally, to talk with hundreds, probably thousands of Indian casino customers. And while certainly there are differences in their experiences at different tribal casinos across the United States, you would be amazed at how similar their comments are. I realize that there are cynics out there who also hear customer comments and would probably like to say that these responses are closer to, "Gimme, gimme" or "The games are fixed," but I can tell you that this is just not true. The wants and needs of Indian gaming customers are much simpler and less thief-like than that.

So I thought that I would share with you the five most common things that Indian gaming customers tell me. Not once, not twice, but over and over and over again. If you are wise, you will heed their words.

"We like our Indian casino" — Yes, it's true. Whether the Indian casino is small or large, located next door or 60 miles away, or has a hundred slots or a few thousand slots, these gamers like their Indian casinos. Sure it's often the only game in town, but these customers tell me they like many of the features of their Indian gaming experience. They like the quality food at inexpensive prices and the fact that there now is entertainment in their often entertainment-starved communities. They like the new multi-line video slot machines. In many states (especially California), they like that there is still a place where they can smoke freely (but conversely, non-smokers are craving significant non-smoking gaming space). What was interesting for me was that customers of alcohol-free Indian casinos say they like casinos dry — fewer drunks and problems. They like the free self-serve coffee and soft drinks on the floor of so many tribal casinos. Yes, your customers like you. And while there are some raising hell about Indian gaming in your communities, it isn't those who have come to love dropping coins in your slot machines. And it may

surprise you, but these customers actually prefer giving their gaming dollars to their Indian neighbors, rather than some big, faceless, out-of-state casino corporation.

"I don't like to wait" — Gaming is a fast-paced activity. The reels spin fast. The cards are dealt fast. Players win or lose fast. This is why your customers like gaming. Their hearts beat faster in anticipation of winning. It is counterproductive to ever make them wait. They've told me they hate to wait — for jackpot payoffs, for hopper fills, for cashing out at the main cashier or change booth, for cocktail service, for service in the buffet. You name it, and your customers hate waiting for it. That's why one of your most powerful marketing strategies can be to eliminate waits, especially on weekends. Of course I know it is difficult to do — regulations, tight labor markets, blah, blah, blah. Just realize, those waits are costing you big bucks!

"Let me win" — Believe me, by now your customers know the score and realize that winning in a casino doesn't come easy (Did you know that 20 percent to 25 percent of your customers leave as winners on an average day?). But it may surprise you that they don't mind losing, if only they can win along the way and play for awhile. They tell me that all the time. It should lead you to address your hold percentages, hit frequencies, bonus opportunities and promotions that can create a sense of winning.

"Be nice" — It's not that your Indian gaming employees aren't nice. Many are, and your customers recognize them, especially those they have come to know well. But your customers tell me about all of those situations where someone didn't smile, someone didn't apologize for a screw-up, someone quoted a stupid regulation for why they couldn't answer a simple request, and yes, when someone was downright rude and treated them as an inconvenience. While getting your employees to be nice is never easy, it gets to the core of your casino company's culture and is also the area that can make a big difference for your guests. How do I know? They told me so!

"Don't take me for granted" — Especially at Indian casinos that have been around awhile, customers give me a lot of feedback about things I loosely lump under the category of "being taken for granted." Sometime it is because they didn't receive an event invitation or a birthday card. But sometimes it is because they see unknown bus customers

getting packages of goodies or senior citizens who never gamble receiving a free meal on Wednesdays. These well intentioned marketing programs lead them to ask, "Hey, what about me? What do I get? I'm here all the time." The lesson there is to be sure that your top 20 percent of customers (who probably account for 60 percent to 70 percent of your Indian gaming revenues) feel that they are being justly rewarded for their frequent visits.

So there you have the heart of the feedback that I have heard from your Indian gaming customers: "We like you." "Let me win." "Be nice." "Don't make me wait." "Don't take me for granted."

Pretty simple, really. Now, as an Indian casino that cares about listening to its customers, what are you going to do about it?

What Indian gaming employees tell me

In a previous issue of *Native American Casino*, I wrote about the kinds of things I continuously hear from Indian casino customers. I found it interesting that across hundreds of different gaming experiences, provided by hundreds of different tribes, the feedback could be so similar.

Well guess what? I have also spent the last three years in my marketing consulting practice, both formally and informally, talking with hundreds, even thousands of your Indian casino employees — both as a marketing researcher looking for answers and a customer looking for a good time. Again, different Indian casinos generate different employee feedback, but the common threads of their responses are strikingly similar.

So allow me to share with you "What your Indian gaming employees tell me." I hope you listen to their united voices and use their words to improve your tribal casino.

"Tell me what's happening" — The communication issue is a common one at all casinos, even all businesses for that matter. Employees want to know that there is a special event next week for invited casino guests. But they also want to know about their department's financial performance. They want to know about decisions made and issues being considered by the tribal council. Often they not only want to know, they want to know *why* — why the new regulation demands their pockets be sewn shut, why they have to clock in 15 minutes early, why they can't smoke anymore on the casino floor. Too often, these employees tell me they are left out of the loop, and then, even when they are included, they are given insufficient explanations. Trust me, you can never give your employees too much information. And all that confidential stuff? How much really needs to be kept from your employees?

"Let me do my job" — The expression of this sentiment takes many different forms. Sometimes it is in employee feedback about their uncomfortable or dorky looking uniforms (Why don't we *always* have the employees choose their own uniforms???). Sometimes it is an expression of frustration over nonsensical regulations that handcuff an employee from serving a customer (three signatures to pay a $250 jackpot?!). Sometimes these employees just want the equipment to do their job right or even the equipment that they do have to *actually work right*. But the

loudest feedback from these Indian gaming employees (both tribal and non-tribal members) involves getting rid of the "slackers" — those employees that are chronically calling in sick, slacking off even when they are there and constantly affecting the morale of the whole department when they are allowed to return to work after being fired two, three or four times. These slackers are not allowing your good employees to do their jobs to the best of their ability. And look, I understand the patience that is necessary to help people who have chronically been unemployed, but when it affects your best employees, you have gone too far.

"Give me help when I need it" — Indian casino employees tell me that they are often overwhelmed and don't get help when they need it. Sometimes this occurs when there is too much business and not enough casino help on weekends. But they also tell me it occurs when they are thrown into roles or situations where they have little or no training. Or when they work in a department desperately in need of some hands-on, on-floor managerial guidance, but their managers are rarely seen on the front line or in the busy casino on weekends.

"Be fair and consistent" — Over and over again, these Indian casino employees tell me that there are some good managers at their casino, but that no two apply the rules the same way and this inconsistency drives them crazy. And while it would be naïve to assume that there are no issues with Indian managers and non-Indian employees or vice versa, many employees tell me that fairness, respect and consistency are much more important in a manager than the color of one's skin or one's cultural background. In fact, there is an interesting amount of support for tribal hiring preference among Indian casino employees, as long as it is administered fairly and communicated well.

"Appreciate me" — By far the loudest refrain among tribal casino employees involves issues of being appreciated for what they do for the Indian gaming organization. And only rarely is this plea heard as a demand for higher wages or better benefits. Only sometimes is it heard as a cry for more and better formal employee recognition or career path programs. But it is *always* heard as a poignant plea for more pats on the back, more "attaboys," more expressions of gratitude for working overtime for the sixth day in a row or getting the job done with a short staff. Yes, your Indian casino employees have not hit me with a long list of monetary de-

mands, but they have overwhelmed me with a simple desire for gratitude on a real human level. You are providing it, aren't you?

Yes, if you take the time to listen to your Indian casino employees, you will hear what I have heard so plainly in the last three years. And if you indeed care about your "New Buffalo," you will take the time to nurture those hunters, those dedicated employees who hunt that New Buffalo for you every day.

Some tips on finding good employees

One of the big issues that I often see in my Indian gaming consulting is how to find and keep good tribal gaming employees. In fact, even with the recent economic downturn, this is an issue that affects numerous businesses in the country, not just Indian casinos. Good folks are just hard to find.

What makes it even more challenging for Indian casinos is that their properties are often in remote locations and require a long commute. They have unique challenges with tribal hiring preference policies. Although many casino jobs pay very well, others are entry-level positions that often have high turnover. And because many casinos are 24-hour businesses, it can be hard to fill those graveyard and swing shifts at the casino. All of these issues and more have created situations where many Indian casinos now have permanent openings for some positions. This certainly threatens the casino's economic well being.

Well I'm here to tell you that the Indian gaming employment situation need not be bleak and that there are several things you can be doing (indeed some casinos are *already* doing) to address this critical need. So allow me to share my tips on finding, keeping, developing and attracting good employees for your tribal casino.

Get everyone involved — The tendency at most casinos is to throw the entire employee recruitment task onto the human resources department and then sit back and complain about the quantity and quality of the applicants received. Sure, the HR folks should provide assistance, but hey, department heads, it's your butts on the line if you can't get enough workers. So start doing you own recruiting and hand out business cards in the community when you see an employee who catches your eye. Have your supervisors and front-line employees do the same, then reward them when they find a new recruit for your department. When I last had a real casino job, I used to have a fold-open business card that said on the inside, "I Noticed You Delivering Great Customer Service." Not only did it help recognize good current employees, but it was a great recruiting tool as well. So start prospecting, because critical needs call for drastic measures and finding employees should be *everyone's* responsibility.

Be creative — Most casinos have a standard set of tactics to get employees — job hotlines, newspaper ads, job fairs, employee referrals, etc. Well there are a whole bunch of other tactics if you just brainstorm the problem. Foxwoods offered a drawing for a new Corvette for employee referrals (Think they got any candidates???). One casino targeted international exchange students. Others have come up with innovative and flexible programs to attract teenagers and senior citizens. At Raving Consulting, when we needed a new employee, we wrote a warm, honest, 450-word ad that got over 100 applicants. And don't be afraid to enlist the help of your marketing department (who else should be better able to *sell?*). At one Midwest casino, the marketing department came up with a successful "Weekend Warrior" program that targeted part-time workers and also did a successful mailing for new employees by targeting the low-end members of its casino database.

Train on the front end — Sometimes the problem isn't finding employees, but rather getting them comfortable with the operation and the organization. I have seen too many situations where new employees are thrown into the fire with little information and little training, and then we wonder why they leave. So invest a little on the front end. It will make more new employees successful and spread positive word of mouth to other potential recruits.

Find out why they're leaving — If you're not asking employees why they leave your Indian gaming organization (exit interviews), you should. You might uncover serious issues that are handicapping you in the race to find and keep good employees.

Don't just automatically spend more money — The tendency when there are no job applicants is to raise the starting wage by a few cents or even a few bucks. Resist this urge, because it will only lead to a bidding war with other casinos or other businesses. Instead, consider unique features that may have more value to potential employees like childcare, flexible benefits, 10-hour shifts, job sharing, etc.

Keep the employees you have — Most of the time we think about the employment situation in terms of finding *new* people. Well, if you can do a better job of keeping the good employees you do have, you won't need near as many new employees. So if you are not listening to your current workers, if you are not providing meaningful recognition to those that are doing a good job right now, if, in short, you are taking your employees for granted, then you need to change that *right now*. For no technique for finding new Indian gaming employees can ever be effective if you are not nurturing those folks that have, and are currently, helping you and your tribal casino reap the benefits of the New Buffalo.

Coming trends in Indian gaming

A while back, a fellow columnist and associate, Jim Rafferty, wrote a column in *Global Gaming Business* about "Mega Trends," big issues that will affect the gaming industry in years to come. It was a look into the crystal ball, and Rafferty made strong cases for the coming importance of technology, coinless gaming, executive training and a host of other things. He suggested that California tribal casinos would be one of the jurisdictions that would dominate the casino expansion news.

Well that got me to thinking. I too have a crystal ball and I have spent much of my last five years working in Indian Country. So what the heck, I thought I'd share with you what I see as coming trends in Indian gaming. Some of them, I believe, may have already started. I may be wrong about others; you may even violently disagree with my predictions. That's OK, I've been wrong before. But where I am right, it may get you thinking about the future of your tribal casino.

Coming trends:

Customer service — As Indian gaming markets mature and competition slows growth, there will be an increased focus on customer service. There will be a shift where tribes begin to work regulations into the customer experience, rather than the customer experience around regulations.

Cheaper slot machines — 1-cent, 2-cent and 5-cent slot machines will dominate most casino floors, and those floors will be more profitable because players will bet numerous coins on numerous lines on these higher hold machines.

Resort development — A new generation of tribal casinos will evolve, with more amenities like hotels, golf courses, theme parks, entertainment centers, etc. For half of the tribes this development will be beneficial, for the other half it will be ill advised.

Direct marketing — Effective direct marketing techniques, to known customers of known worth (direct mail, e-mail, telemarketing, voice messaging, etc.), will supplant at least 50 percent of current advertising expenses, as advertising will increasingly be seen as expensive and immeasurable.

Bingo and keno slide — Bingo and keno will continue their slow decline at tribal casinos and the only profitable bingo operations will be at tribal casinos offering huge payouts (for large crowds) and those casinos leveraging more profitable (and more fun) bingo machines.

Problem gambling — Continued lawsuits against casinos by problem gamblers will prompt an aggressive and unified response from tribal casinos across the United States. This effort will be led by the National Indian Gaming Association (NIGA) and will involve more awareness, more training, some funding of treatment organizations and a standardized code of conduct.

Coinless gaming — In five years, all machines at all tribal casinos will be coinless and ticket-in/ticket-out will be standard. Gamblers will embrace this convenience, realizing it gives them *more time in action*.

Competition — Indian gaming will face the threat of increased competition as card clubs, racetracks, charities and others continue to make political noise, no longer to stop Indian gaming, but to chime in on their benefits.

Table game business increase — There will be a marked increase in table game play as the number of gambling Gen-Xers (who love tables) continues to grow and tribes continue to find ways to make the table game experience more fun and more attractive.

Non-smoking gaming space — There will be a significant increase in quality, non-smoking gaming areas at casinos as societal pressure continues to build and customers demand it. Tribes will notice increased revenues from this change as more non-smokers are attracted to casinos.

Communities — The trend of non-Indian communities supporting their local tribal casino will continue to grow as peoples' stereotypes of casinos diminish and their understanding of the benefits of Indian gaming for their own communities expands.

Selling the casino — A powerful sales training trend will take over the entire gaming industry where gaming employees will actively show customers how to spend more money at other casino games and amenities, increasing guest enjoyment and spending.

Compacts — Texas, Florida, Nebraska and Oklahoma tribes will all sign gaming compacts with their states' governors. Hey, I can wish big if I want. After all, right or wrong, these are my visions of the future.

If I ran an Indian casino

In the three-plus years that I have been a gaming marketing consultant, I have worked with over 30 Indian gaming organizations and learned about many more from my students at a variety of seminars and presentations that I have conducted. In addition, several friends and associates have held senior management positions at several tribal casinos and have shared much feedback about their various experiences. I have also spoken with thousands of Indian casino customers and employees, both tribal and non-tribal, in the course of my consulting work and customer experience at Indian casinos.

All of this combined doesn't make me an expert on Indian gaming, but I feel it does allow me to make the following observations. I hope you find my thoughts and observations to be valuable for your tribal casino.

If I ran an Indian casino, I would:

- Have each non-tribal member of my management team take one-week indoctrinations on the history and culture of the tribe for whom they are going to work. This session would be mandatory and would need to be completed before the executive could begin work;

- Ask our tribal council to throw a welcome party for each new senior executive of our management team and have the council members and managers bring their entire families to the party;

- Spend at least half of my working time on the casino floor interacting with customers and employees;

- Establish a harmonious working relationship with the tribal gaming commission and stress to them that we are all on the same team;

- Review every rule, regulation and procedure to see how it might be improved, without compromising the casino's integrity, to enhance the customer's experience;

- Immediately reduce the advertising budget by at least 50 percent;

- Conduct periodic meetings with a customer advisory board (made up solely of customers) to hear how they wanted me to run their casino;

- Have every employee carry business cards to be used for recruiting new customers and new employees;

- Meet with every non-tribal community organization to explain who we are and ask how we might be able to develop mutually beneficial activities. I would invite them to lunch at the casino and offer them a free yearly slot tournament (they recruit the players) for their organization;

- Conduct every new hire orientation myself and make it a celebration. I would include significant pieces on customer service, tribal history and culture, tribal preference hiring policy and *why* it is important and the goals of the casino organization;

- Have every manager work on weekends — when most of our customers are there;

- Meet with employees continuously and solicit and reward their suggestions for improving the casino experience;

- Have our managers spend 80 percent of their working time with their *good* employees;

- Pay our most important customer contact positions — slot club rep, valet parking attendant, front desk clerk, etc. — as if they were the most important. I would create a career path among these positions for my friendliest employees;

- Spend the bulk of our *marketing* dollars on the customers who were spending their *gambling* dollars at our casino;

- Have bus business come to the casino only if it was during the weekdays and didn't upset our regular customers;

- Position our casino as a regional entertainment destination and become known as "the place" to go for a night out;

- Have a *great* buffet restaurant that included recipes from our customers;

- Have our other restaurants be franchises of the *best* regional restaurants in our area;

- Insist that our dealers spend as much time practicing their customer interactions as their physical dealing skills;

- Allow our regular customers to get a "peek behind the curtain" and visit the surveillance and count rooms;

- Ensure that all supervisors are telling our employees daily when they do a good job;

- Let our employees choose their own benefits from a menu of benefits;

- Allow the employees to decide if and how they want an employee of the month program;

- Create a customer of the month program;

- Have a player's club that gives customers credit any place where they can spend money (hotel, shows, retail, gaming, etc.) and allow them to define their own types of player benefits;

- Make guest service and greeting of customers the most important job of our security officers;

- Be sure to have enough employees working on weekends, so that service was actually better than during the week;

- Visit the local tribal community organization frequently to understand the benefit from the tribal gaming profits;

- Insist on at least one week of customer service training for every employee, every year;

- Have our best customers do customer service shopping for our casino;

- Instruct our managers to be customers at all of our competitors' casinos at least four times per year;

- Develop a meaningful, ongoing management development program for qualified tribal members; and

- Fire myself within five years and replace me with the most qualified tribal gaming executive.

Yes, if I ran an Indian casino, it would be unlike any that you or your customers have ever seen. Exactly.

What the casino industry can learn from Indian gaming

Having cut my teeth in the traditional gaming markets, it has been interesting for me over the last three years of my consulting business to watch and participate in the growth and development of Indian gaming. Even before I got involved with working with Native American gaming tribes, I had read some of the inflammatory stories and heard some of the industry whispering.

"Indian casinos are poorly regulated and will give the gaming industry a black eye."

"Customers should be concerned about getting ripped off at an Indian casino."

"Indians don't know how to run a casino."

Well I've got news for these old-school gaming naysayers. Either the gaming business is not hard to run after all, or Native Americans are a quick study. Because Indian casinos are not only up and running, they are thriving. So much so that old-time gamers could now learn a thing or two from our Indian brethren.

Yes, it's true. There is much to learn from the growth of Indian gaming, and not just how to overcome adversity. Although that, I'm sure, is a valuable lesson.

So allow me to share with you, what I think the gaming industry could learn from Indian gaming. Will it listen? From my experience, probably not, but all the more power to Indian gaming!

Community involvement — Most casinos support their local communities, but only Indian gaming supports both tribal and non-tribal communities. And it is not just cash donations. Indian casinos are actively *involved* and making a big difference. Whether it's in building tribal community or service centers, providing seed money for new tribal enterprises or a variety of other significant involvements, Indian gaming has shown the traditional gaming industry how to take community support to community *commitment*. The non-Indian gaming industry just typically throws dollars at a few pet projects of a senior gaming executive.

Playing the political game — In general, the entire gaming industry has gotten much better at representing its political interest, as witnessed by the growth of both NIGA and the AGA. But Indian gaming's political interests are often about *survival* of its gaming enterprise, so its response often needs to be fast and significant. One needs only to look at California tribes' Proposition 5 and Proposition 1A campaigns to realize how masterful Indian casinos have become at the political game. Add to that Indian gaming response to tax and sovereignty threats, efforts to achieve federal recognition and influence leveraged in state and local elections, and I think you would have to agree that Indian gamers have been more effective than their traditional counterparts with their traditional "government relations" executives.

Sensitivity to alcohol — Alcohol is a little discussed issue in the gaming industry, but it is one of its perceived Achilles heels. The perception of casinos plying gamblers with free or cheap whisky, whether unfair or not, definitely exists with the public, even if it is only with the anti-gambling public. The numerous examples of Indian casinos with "no alcohol" or "limited alcohol" policies help to counteract this negative image and set a new gaming industry standard. This is even more impressive, given that gaming tribes response to this issue is entirely *voluntary*, whereas traditional gamers only come to this progressive alcohol policy when it is *mandated.*

Learning and development — Indian gamers are much more open to learning and much more committed to executive development than their traditional counterparts. Sure, one could say they *have to be* more committed because they are so new to the business, but it is my belief that this stems from a deeper, core cultural belief about gaining wisdom to build long-term value for tribal people. In the traditional gaming world, learning is valued more as a cold, clinical, profit-generating or career propelling tool.

Employment as a goal — I don't know of one traditional casino that has as one of its goals to "keep people employed." In fact, at the first business downturn, they are quick to cut staff. But I know of many tribal casinos that will sacrifice profits to keep tribal members employed. It just seems so much more of a human approach, even if no corporate casino would ever consider it.

Standing tall when right — Indian gamers stand stubborn and tall when right. Whether it is against encroachments of tribal sovereignty or just to do the right thing in a local community dispute, there can be no mistaking the steel will of the gaming tribes. And who can blame them? Who else will stand up for them?

Yes, there is already much to learn from the Indian gaming experience. I only hope that we can all overcome our narrowness and our prejudices to indeed learn it.

Qualities of great general managers

My consulting work has brought me into close contact with literally hundreds of casinos, including scores of tribal casinos. It certainly has been a learning experience. And although I have had significant interactions with hundreds of casino executives in these different casinos, they certainly have not been distributed equally.

For instance, I haven't spent too much time with security directors or food and beverage directors or CFOs (unless they misplace my invoices). No, I have spent a disproportionate amount of my consulting time with marketing, gaming and human resources executives — and with GMs.

General managers of casinos are an interesting group. There is really no one style that categorizes them and they typically have wildly different backgrounds and levels of experience (although one thing that is consistent among them, in my opinion, is that there are *way too few* female general managers of casinos).

As far as tribal casinos go, I think Indian gaming in general has proven that you do not need to have 20 years of experience, or have worked in Las Vegas, or have been a table games manager to be an effective general manager. And certainly tribal members, with the right experience and the right qualities can be extremely effective in the "head honcho" position. I know; I have seen it many times. Tribal casino self-management can indeed be a reality.

And that got me to thinking about what makes a great general manager. Is it training? Is it ability to understand budgets? Strategic thinking skills? What?

So I have looked at the great general managers with whom I have come into contact (including several GMs of Indian casinos), and here's my take on the common qualities that make them *great*. Certainly, effective management styles of these GMs can vary and some of them may not possess every single quality, but I believe that there are certainly many of these common traits shared by all of them.

Qualities of great general managers:

They continually think from the customer and employee perspective — Sure, they manage against budgets and ratios and standards, but they know that the casino business is all about *people*.

They have the ability to think out of the box and continually ask, "What if?" — What if we had "Welcome" signs at our casino entrances instead of "Warning" signs? What if we found a way for our customers not to wait in line when the restaurants are busy? What if …?

They are approachable — They don't hide their office behind a "Restricted Access" door or a gauntlet of administrative support staff whose job is to screen who gets the privilege of seeing the big cheese. They are often on the casino floor and employees and customers feel comfortable in approaching them … and vice versa.

They understand marketing — They know that marketing is not advertising, or buses or entertainment, but an integrated "way of doing business" that breeds loyalty and word of mouth referrals. They understand the power of the 20/80 rule that 20 percent of customers typically account for 80 percent of a casino's profitability.

They are passionate about great customer service — And they are not afraid to spend some money around hiring, training, research and reward/recognition to ensure that they get it.

They react to crises, bad news and screw ups with a cool head — They don't overreact and their "cool heads" keep all managers and employees calm and understanding that "this too shall pass."

They allow their managers to run their own departments — They don't micromanage, meddle or second-guess. They know they have hired competent people for executive positions and they have the confidence in them to run their own world.

They have an appreciation, but not a preoccupation with budget numbers — They are not bean counters, but they understand the importance of staying within budget. However, their orientation is to "manage to their customers" and have the budgets logically follow, rather than vice versa.

They continually look into the future — And they anticipate where future business will come from, what might happen if competition enters the market and how to plan for the development of senior gaming executives to run the business 10 years down the road.

They have an understanding and appreciation of the tribal perspective — And although they may not be a tribal member themselves, these great GMs have knowledge of a tribe's history, an understanding of a tribe's sovereignty and clear buy-in to a tribe's goals and vision.

So there you have it, my thoughts on truly *great* general managers. And, if your GM is not quite there yet, that's OK, because it certainly is a lofty goal and a never-ending process of improvement. But where it occurs, you will see happy employees, satisfied customers and a thriving Indian gaming business. Yes, a great GM can make that much of a difference.

Topics rarely discussed

Part of the work of being a consultant is digging below the surface of issues and getting to the root causes so that leverage points can be identified and real solutions can be produced.

But it ain't easy digging deeper into gaming organizations, whether they're tribal or non-tribal ones. You're never sure what you are going to find and oftentimes the client doesn't want to go there.

Some examples:

Sometimes a general manager might want to fix his casino's customer service (which might be lacking), but the real problem could be the GM's top-down, autocratic leadership style that will not allow employees to make those decisions that could positively affect the customer experience.

Occasionally a marketing director will bemoan a viciously competitive gaming market where it becomes more and more necessary to "buy the business" when the real problem might be the marketing director's unwillingness to talk to her customers … or an unreasonable belief in advertising as a chief marketing tactic.

A casino department head might bemoan "the tight labor market" or "human resources always sending me poor candidates" when the real problem might be the department head's inability to recruit, train or motivate.

A player's club manager might complain about the poor support from the slot system manufacturer when the real problem might be the manager's uneasiness with technology.

Sometimes what you see isn't what you get.

Now my work with tribal casinos for the most part has been extremely gratifying and I enjoy seeing Native American people make economic progress at long last. But I would be less than honest if I didn't tell you that it is sometimes frustrating getting to the root issues at some Indian casinos, just like it is at some traditional casinos.

When I think back on these situations and try to identify some common factors at work, it appears that these deeper issues often lie in a few key areas in the tribal gaming system. So if you are struggling with your tribal gaming business and want to understand where the problems *really* might be, you might want to look here:

The surrounding non-tribal communities — Sure, many communities have embraced their new "gaming entertainment," but let's face it, racism is still alive and well in this country. Strong anti-gaming sentiment also still exists in many places. Ignorance about tribal sovereignty is widespread — just ask a few members of your local communities if Indian gaming profits should be taxed! These attitudes can certainly cause problems for your Indian casino and while the tendency might be to throw money at a few local charities or politicians, the real answer might be in community education and relationship-building efforts.

The GM's office — Yes, I know that there are many talented and capable executives (both tribal and non-tribal ones) in Indian gaming. Heck, I have worked with many of them. But I can also tell you that there are a few lacking some critical skills to be effective GMs. There are a few who don't give a hoot about Native Americans or their culture. There are a few who think they are running a prison instead of a "gaming entertainment" place where customers are supposed to have *fun*. There are even a few who dislike gaming and all of the people (often referred to as "suckers") who participate in it. And just like in traditional gaming, there have always been a few senior executives who are in their position because of *who* they know instead of *what* they know. So sometimes while you are paying for "departmental efficiency audits," your greatest efficiency may come with one simple personnel move.

The tribal gaming commission — Of course I realize that there are numerous talented, hard-working tribal gaming regulators who perform an essential and often thankless task at their Indian casino. But I have also seen the occasional individual who appears to be off on a power trip and takes great glee in nailing the gaming operators on even the most minor of infractions. Just think how great these individuals would be if they could spend some of that law enforcement energy on finding ways to help gaming departments work better together for the benefit of the customer.

The tribal council — There's no question that serving on a tribal council can be an extremely difficult and politically-charged task. Tribal council members also tend to be the most talented and caring members of their organization. Often they do a great job of steering their tribal gaming enterprise. But I have also seen a few examples of tribal councils micromanaging their casino, sending fired employees (sometimes relatives) back to work for a fourth or fifth time (over the objections of their casino managers) or forcing decisions on how to spend tribal profits that could threaten the casino's long-term health.

Yes, it's true we do not always like to confront the deeper issues in the gaming industry. But by doing so, you may well keep your Indian gaming business not only strong, but also true to the goals of your tribal people.

Dealing with sensitive issues

We know well that being in the gaming business involves dealing with some sensitive issues. Some people absolutely oppose gaming on purely moral grounds. Some people cannot deal with the gaming experience without going overboard. Handling local communities can raise certain challenges. There are the typical occupational hazards and environmental issues — smoke, noise, traffic, environmental impact, etc. And of course, the whole regulatory aspect of casinos raises issues of honesty, corruption and fairness.

No, it is not easy running a modern-day casino and dealing with these many sensitive issues on a day-to-day basis.

Being that Indian gaming is relatively new, it has been interesting for me to observe how the various tribes have addressed these sticky problems in their gaming business. In many cases I have been impressed, while in others, somewhat disappointed.

Let me share my thoughts on how I see gaming tribes dealing with some of these thorny, sensitive issues that surround gaming:

Investment in tribal communities:

Here I think that Indian gaming operators overall have done a fantastic job. There is always a challenge in figuring out how best to spend gaming profits. Make per cap payments? Reinvest in the casino? Build more resources for the tribal community? From what I have seen, Indian gaming tribes have handled this often contentious and politically-charged process well and have managed the balancing act of building their tribal communities while they also build their business.

Interaction with non-tribal local communities:

Let's face it. This is not a very easy task. Many in the local communities have opposed and continue to oppose Indian gaming. Sometimes it is jealousy. Sometimes it is fear. Sometimes it is plain racism. But whatever the reason, opposition has always existed in some quarters in the communities surrounding Indian gaming operations. But I do believe that tribal operators have increasingly handled this situation well. Key donations have been made to influential community organizations. Tribes have successfully organized themselves politically. Community events are conducted at Indian casinos. Educational efforts have been launched to have communities understand all of the benefits brought by tribal gaming. Innovative programs have been launched (a` la Lake of the Torches' "Community Cash" program) that stimulate business activity in non-tribal communities. Partnerships have been created. Yes, I believe that tribes have made great progress on this issue, but much more remains to be done.

Alcohol policy:

This is one area where I believe that Indian casino operators have set a new standard for the industry. Who would have thought that you could have casinos with no alcohol and have customers say that they like it that way? That is the case at many Indian casinos. At others, alcohol is not given away, but sold at the request of the gaming customer. These responsible alcohol policies should serve as a model to the rest of the gaming industry who continue to be portrayed as bad guys who ply their customers with alcohol and then take their money.

Smoke:

Here is where I feel that tribal gaming operators have a big opportunity. Only 25 percent to 30 percent of the population smokes. Smoke in the workplace continues to be a big issue. Tobacco lawsuits have started to assign blame for smoking related causes. Yet, from my journeys though Indian casinos, I can tell you that non-smoking areas are still no more than slight token gestures. Sure, some bingo rooms have separate, pretty well-ventilated non-smoking areas, but most Indian casinos only pay lip service to this issue on their main gaming floor. The answer here is to make a significant commitment, stick with that commitment and proudly shout it out to your customers. Don't just take an under performing casino area, throw up a few signs and call it a non-smoking zone.

Problem gambling:

I will first confess my bias here, in that I have been active on the problem gambling issue for over 10 years and I believe that the gaming industry proactively needs to address it. And I do believe that great strides have been made in raising awareness of this sensitive issue and marshalling resources to address it. That having been said, I believe that in Indian Country, dealing with this issue has been too much on a casino-by-casino basis, rather than a concerted effort among concerned tribes from the same states or regions of the country. In Nevada, we did not learn to make progress on the problem gambling front until the casino operators first joined together, second made a significant financial commitment and third, partnered with organizations that could provide resources to assist problem gamblers and their families. The same process, I believe, needs to take place in Indian gaming to a greater degree than it currently has.

So there you have my report card on Indian gaming's response to some sensitive gaming issues: great at dealing with their communities and leading the way on the alcohol issue, with room for improvement on the smoking and problem gambling fronts. And as I believe Indian gaming tribes have a more ingrained sensitivity than their traditional gaming counterparts, I have no doubts that great strides will continue to be made on these issues that are so important to us all.

I have a dream

I am your Indian gaming customer. And I have a dream.

In my dream, I arrive at your Indian casino and your valet parker greets me by name and welcomes me back. He opens the car door for both my wife and me, washes my windshield and offers each of us a mint. He then tells us about the special items in the buffet and wishes us good luck.

In my dream, as I enter the casino I notice all the signs and words of welcome and I see pictures of the smiling faces of all the lucky people who have won jackpots at your casino. I see more smiling faces of your employees in plaques honoring their "heroism" in serving guests. I don't see one sign telling me what I can't do, or what all your rules are, or how you can ask me to leave for any reason if you wish to. Then, almost by magic, a security officer opens the door for me, welcomes me to your casino, wishes me luck and tells me the progressive bonus at the 25-cent video poker machine bank near the cage is over $1,500 and "due to hit any time now."

In my dream, I approach your players club booth and I'm once again welcomed by name. Without asking, your players club representative tells me about your double points promotion for the rest of the day and that I currently have six comp dollars and four cash-back dollars in my account. She asks me if I need another players club card for my wife because she notices that she left it in the slot machine on her last visit. Then she tells me to look for a special birthday offer next month and that your casino "is a great place to spend a birthday!"

In my dream, I sit down to play my favorite video poker machine and I am immediately approached by one of your gaming "hosts" and once again greeted by name — it's amazing how many of your staff know my name. I'm impressed how your hosts can do anything for me, and I mean *anything* — get me a drink or a snack, make change, fix my machine, make dinner reservations, arrange to get my car brought out at valet parking — *anything*! Why, at most casinos it takes four or five different employees to do all that and you do it with a single host!

In my dream, I go to a podium to make blackjack reservations for 5:00 p.m. with Larry, my favorite dealer, on the double-deck, $25 minimum, $1,000 maximum bet table. It's great how you let me choose the type of game I like to play with the dealers I like best. I wish more casinos would do that. And I really like how your floor people ask players if they would like to have new decks of cards put on a game or if they want to keep the same "lucky" cards for another hour. Most places just dump the new cards on the game without a word — sometimes they even do it on a whim, just because the players are finally winning a few bucks.

In my dream, I check into my hotel room in your VIP express line and there is absolutely zero paperwork. Once again the clerk welcomes me by name, hands me my key and tells me that I can go straight to my room and my bags will be there in less than five minutes. And it's only 8:30 a.m.! When I ask why check-in for rooms isn't at 3:00 p.m. or 4:00 p.m. like it is at most casino hotels, your office manager explains that you figured out long ago how to build your check-in process around your guests instead of your room-cleaning schedule.

When I arrive at my room, it is nice to get a call from a gaming host, welcoming me by name, asking if I need anything and inviting me to the afternoon reception hosted by the general manager. Boy does that make me feel special! And when I look around the room, I see the magazines I like to read, a bag of Cheetos (my favorite!) and some complimentary Academy Award-winning videos to watch in the evening. How did you know I just love "One Flew Over the Cuckoo's Nest?!"

In my dream, I eat at your casino's restaurants. I don't know how you do it, but I never see what I see at other casinos — long lines and empty tables. Your food is great. I love how your chef shares his favorite recipes with the guests and then, in reverse, how he features special guest recipes on the buffet menu. And I *love* how your food servers all suggest which wines will go well with my meal and how they allow me to try tiny samples of those decadent desserts — you know, I always have one, I just can't help myself after I taste it. And oh, by the way, thanks for figuring out how to never have me wait for the check, so I can get back to gambling quicker!

Yes, I have a dream, and in it, your casino experience is all about *me* — what I like, what I need, what I want. Not about rules … or staffing levels … or profits. But about *me*. Shouldn't that be what your Indian casino experience is all about? You can make my dream a reality, if you want to. Then I will have no reason to go anywhere else but to *your* Indian casino, which I will call "*mine*."

The customer vs. the commission

It is a valid and important goal of your Indian gaming organization to have effective regulations and procedures in place to protect the assets of the tribe and maintain the confidence of the gaming public. Likewise, it is important to give excellent service in an Indian casino and to have effective marketing programs in place, to ensure that there is a steady flow of satisfied customers which will make the gaming enterprise thrive.

However, sometimes the goals of "serving the commission" and "serving the customer" can come into conflict. In these situations, a decision must often be made as to what is more important, how the gaming commission's regulations should be enforced or how user friendly the guest experience should be when encountering these commission rules. Too often, I'm afraid, casino management automatically sides with the commission over the customer. Let me give you some real life examples that I have seen:

The NIGC mandate:

When the National Indian Gaming Commission (NIGC) first began promulgating a standard set of recommended regulatory guidelines for tribal casinos in the United States, one of the issues that it felt needed addressing was what to do with players club cards that were abandoned in slot machines. The NIGC felt that it was a conflict for these cards to be returned to the players club, since it was the card issuer as well as the redemption area for accrued points on those cards. So the NIGC recommended that security should handle these lost cards and that if they were not claimed within 24 hours, they should be destroyed. But the unintended consequences of this policy were to give security a task it did not want, to send customers to an intimidating place to recover from their simple absent-mindedness (and which ran counter to their intuition as to where to retrieve their cards) and to increase the casino's costs of making players club cards. Some empathy for the customer experience might have led to a different and more effective regulation.

Controlling drawing tickets like cash:

One tribal casino's gaming commission felt that it was important to administer its big prize giveaways fairly, for after all, you don't want a customer winning the red Camaro (or the house or the $10,000) who hadn't fairly earned their drawing ticket. So they created some regulations and procedures for the distribution of drawing tickets to minimize the chance of a coupon scammer winning the top prize. Drawing tickets had to be filled out in great detail and contain a customer signature. Slot employees needed a security officer to verify the winning event and the handing out of the drawing ticket. Security had to deposit the completed ticket in the drawing drum. So although customers had no complaints about "lookie-loos" winning the promotion prizes, they did hate waiting at the machine to get their drawing ticket (and couldn't play their machine during this time!) and truth be told, they wondered if their ticket actually got put in the drawing drum since they didn't deposit it themselves.

The sewn pockets:

There had been some employee theft at this tribal casino, so the gaming commission decided to "plug the holes" in part by creating a new regulation that mandated all casino cash-handling employees would have all of their pockets sewn shut. While theft was reduced, table game employees spoke about lowered morale and the perception that "no one trusts us any more." Female dealers also complained about having to carry their lunch money in their bras, since pockets were no longer useful (and of course purses couldn't be brought into the pit area).

The cage that couldn't:

This large tribal casino had two separate table game areas with nearly a hundred yards between them. The main area, near the front door, received most of the table game action and because the gaming commission wanted to keep close control of all $500 chips, it established a regulation that only the main cashier cage could cash out $500 chips. Any guests attempting to cash out at the satellite cages with these '"pink" chips were instructed to take them to the far end of where they were, no matter how inconvenient that might be and no matter that each cage had plenty of cash to redeem these high-denomination chips.

I have many more examples of regulations that pit the needs of the commission against the needs of the customers. But I think you get the point. By no means am I suggesting that reasonable rules, regulations and procedures are not important to your tribal gaming operation. But what I think I am suggesting is that it is more than appropriate for you to ask your gaming commission to consider the guest when they are formulating their rules. In fact, you might ask them to role play how the guest will experience a new procedure, or have them meet with groups of guests to get their feedback on how a new regulation might affect them if put into place.

You just might create more effective regulations that will have your gaming commissioners congratulated for their guest focus, and procedures that will leave your guests free to do more gambling, with less time needed to fulfill some "too intrusive" requirements.

Sounds like a win-win to me!

Listening to your Indian gaming customers

I have written and spoken often about the need to listen to customers. It is a fundamental truth — the better you listen to your customers (and then respond to their wants), the more successful your Indian casino will be.

Find out what your customers want, then give it to them. This truth is not only basic, it is also widely accepted. I have never had even one person dispute this notion.

Then why do so many do such a poor or incomplete job of listening to their customers???

While I'm not sure of all the reasons why, I do feel the answer to this lack of customer listening is similar to why so many well-meaning, God-fearing people sin against their own beliefs on a daily basis.

It must be hard listening to casino customers. Or we'd all be doing it.

To shed some light on this listening issue, I thought it might be helpful to list some of the various ways, both formal and informal, of listening to customers. A brief description, followed by a few pros and cons of each tactic is also included. So here are my "Customer Listening Tactics:"

Just talking to 'em — Now here's a simple tactic that involves nothing more than going down on the casino floor and just talking with customers. And it is something that none of us do enough of. It's cheap (unless you overprice the value of your casino executives' time) and highly enlightening. The problem is that most casino executives don't like talking with customers, aren't very good at it or don't know what to ask. Many will say they are too busy to do this simple listening exercise, but that is just a smokescreen for misplaced priorities.

Customer focus groups — These are the small group meetings (six to 10 people per group) where a moderator gets customers to 'fess up how they feel about various aspects of the casino. They can be somewhat costly if you are not able to use your own moderator, and you can jump to wrong conclusions from such small groups, but generally this is powerful stuff and it's heard right from the mouths of your own customers.

Satisfaction surveys — These surveys are meant to reach large numbers of casino customers to inquire about their experience at your casino. They can be done by mail or the telephone, by e-mail or on the

Internet, or by live, on-property interviews. All methods have a certain cost associated with them and each have their own shortcomings (e.g. on mail surveys you can never be sure who completed the form), but they do get you opinions from a lot of folks. Management tends to be more confident in feedback and results from these types of surveys since they are broader based and have a consistent format.

Customer advisory boards — These are interesting listening tactics that are similar to focus groups, but here the customers almost become another arm of management. They give you their feedback with the clear understanding that you will implement their recommendations, and they will expect to have you report back on your progress. This is a powerful tool and is cost effective, but is probably meant only for casinos well down the road to customer worship.

Feedback from employees — If you bother to ask them, employees can give you loads of information on what guests are saying. Just be sure you listen and filter closely, as sometimes personal agendas are involved. It's amazing how dealers who hate smokers will tell you that customers have been complaining about smoke, for example.

Guest comment cards — This is the most common listening post at most casinos. Comment cards are put in hotel rooms, in the restaurants, at the players' club, sometimes on a rack in the middle of the casino, where it quickly starts gathering stray glasses and ashtrays. Comment cards get you some interesting feedback, but it tends to come from super happy or super disgruntled customers, so the true picture can get distorted. Unfortunately, most casinos hang their hat on this customer listening tactic as the only tool that they think they need.

There are other techniques you can use to investigate your Indian casino customer's experience (secret shoppers, use of casino surveillance systems, informal "eavesdropping," etc.). They all can help you listen through your customers' ears and see through your customers' eyes. But what tactics should you use? Good question.

From my experience, it is not so important as to how you listen to your customers, but that you do listen to your customers … regularly, consistently and with a sympathetic ear. For whether it's a simple comment card or a fancy focus group, your "listening to your customer" tactics won't amount to a hill of beans if you are not using their pointed and powerful feedback to improve your Indian gaming operation.

Casino Culture ~ Customer Service

Service as a marketing tool

I have yet to meet a casino executive who didn't (at least intuitively) understand that improving customer service would improve his or her casino's financial results. Therefore, it's very surprising to me that few of these same operators have effective, coordinated customer service programs — and certainly not customer service *cultures* at their casinos. Cost structures, margins, staffing ratios, ROIs, regulatory compliance and other bean counter measurements continue to hold sway over guest satisfaction scores.

Oh sure, Harrah's "gets it" — witness its service protocols for its Diamond- and Platinum-level customers, its Target Patron Satisfaction Surveys (opinions of VIPs drive policy), its frontline employee bonuses for improving service scores, its extensive service training. Heck, its CEO is a former Harvard prof who pioneered the study of the "Service Profit Chain" and the business results achieved by outstanding service providers.

But beyond a few other casino companies and properties (Isle of Capri, Barona, a handful of locals casinos, etc.) the casino industry record of service is pretty spotty. I wouldn't rate overall casino customer service as awful (banks, hospitals and most airlines are *awful*), but I would call it mediocre. High rollers and big tippers will actually get pretty good service and regular customers in a locals casino (unless they're "fleas") will also get treated reasonably well by casino employees. The sad part as I see it, however, is that in a business (gaming) designed to slowly but surely take people's money, the mathematics of losing cries out for a compensatory tactic of *great* service.

I mean, if it was *your* casino (and for many tribal members it *is*) what would your customer service be like??? Shoot, I would just love these crazy gamblers to death!

So I'm mystified. Why aren't casinos second only to Disneyland as the happiest places on earth? Why is customer service training one of the first budget items cut when business slows (if even there *was* any customer service training to cut)? Why are guest satisfaction scores seldom used as a significant component to determine casino executives' bonuses?

Why? Why? Why? Why?

Well, I've thought about why customer service is so misunderstood and underappreciated. Business schools don't teach it. Service is hard to measure and link to a profitable result (but it *can* be done). It costs money. It's a never-ending training battle. Casino customers can be difficult as they lose their money. The casino environment is non-stop, smoky, noisy and repetitive … blah, blah, blah, blah, blah.

Rather than focus on the difficulties of providing great casino customer service (the *excuses* why you don't), let's assume you agree with me that service is lackluster, improving it would help your casino business and you're open to some suggestions for giving your service a shot in the arm. Okay, you're with me so far (and not cussing me out for this "warm and fuzzy crap"). Try this.

First, develop a service goal and strategy and involve every single senior executive to do so, even if you have to drag them kicking and screaming. It ain't gonna happen if you farm the initiative out to human resources or marketing — employees can sniff out the "Cheshire Cat" programs; all smile and no body.

Second, put together a budget for your service improvement efforts — a *sizable* budget. What, you thought you just had to put out a memo and ask your employees to smile more often? What are you, crazy??? What about money for recruiting service minded employees? Money for service training at orientation throughout the year or when employees get promoted to supervisor roles? What about money for the recognition programs? Money to evaluate service in satisfaction surveys, shopper surveys, employee surveys? I'll bet you're beginning to see the need for "shifting budget priorities."

Third, create a position of "Vice President of Service" (not "Services," that is an operational title) and make it second only to the general manager or CEO position. This VP of service would be charged solely with making casino guests happy and service so good "they'd never want to leave." Heck, rotate your current management team through this VP position, then you could ship out those who wanted to stay safe in their budgets and their ratios and their win per units. Hey, we're in a *people* business!

Next, talk to your customers and find out every point of contact with your casino that frustrates them, annoys them, confuses them and pisses them off (trust me, you already know 90 percent of this). Long lines at the cage, sneering/scolding dealers, smoky environments, casino floors that are too hot or too cold, tight machines (*especially*, tight machines), weak benefits for loyal players, etc., etc., etc. Now go out and fix every one of these "guest dissatisfiers." "What?" you say. "I can't fix those long lines at the cage on Saturday nights!" Hire more people. Train your existing people better. Get those cage supervisors off their duffs and working a window. Get rid of one of those ineffective ads or billboards and start your "Cage Service Marketing Program" to delight guests with *something that truly matters to them*! You get the picture. Improve their experience and get them spending less time in line. Hey, a result even a CFO would love!

Finally, when you have done all this (and created effective measurements and rewards and listening posts and service teams and suggestion programs and…), when *finally* you have done all this, be prepared to do more, to do it all over again, to start over, to tweak, to change, to be frustrated, to question whether it's all worth it and to throw more stuff into the fan because great casino customer service is not the result of a program or an incentive or even a great service leader. It's the common realization among your management team that there is nothing more valuable than giving your customers what they want — making it easier for them to do business with you and give you more of their money. Believe it.

Smoke gets in your eyes

It's time to take on another industry sacred cow — non-smoking gaming space. I can see my e-mail inbox filling up already.

First, let me paint the "conventional wisdom" picture of non-smoking casino space. It goes something like this:

(Ms. Slot Director): "I'd love to offer more non-smoking machines. I know it is one of the loudest complaints that I hear from my players and common sense tells me that I should do it, especially since 70 percent of the adult population doesn't smoke! But you know what? Every time I increase the non-smoking slot floor, the win per unit goes in the dumper in that area and the non-smokers still play the machines in the smoking area! Those crazy customers say they want clean air, then they run to the smokiest parts of the joint!"

Other defenders of the conventional wisdom make other spirited points. "Look what happened in Delaware … and Australia. Business went down 20 percent when an entire non-smoking policy was mandated!" Or in California (especially) you'll hear, "These are the last public indoor places in the state where you *can* smoke and now you want the tribes to give up that competitive advantage???"

I'll admit casino examples of good strategic division of smoking and non-smoking gaming space are rare. The current typical model for non-smoking gaming space in Casino Land is a small, cramped space in the least-trafficked corner of the casino. Signage is usually poor there and either secondhand smoke is still present (from the surrounding smoking floor) or enforcement is lax for offending smokers who wander in there, further polluting the concept. Clearly the gaming industry response to non-smoking gaming is a token one.

But there are lights in the tunnel! Crown Casino in Melbourne, without being mandated, offered a spacious, popular non-smoking area that people actually sought out (plus it contained all the games that were in the smoking area). Win-River Casino in Redding, Calif. went from a first generation facility with no significant non-smoking areas to a spanking new facility that was 70 percent smoke-free. And Tabcorp in Australia, after initially taking a revenue hit when a no-smoking policy was state mandated in Australia, has seen revenues start to bounce back as it has found ways to cater to the needs of smoking gamblers (convenient smoking areas off the floor, a policy of holding machines for players to take "smoke breaks," training of employees to understand smokers' needs, etc.).

As one who has talked to thousands of casino customers, formally and informally, I can tell you that "smoky space" is their second-biggest complaint after "tight machines." And it is not just the non-smokers who have this issue. Sometimes the smoke is too much even for smokers, and they dislike being frowned at when they do light up. So, as a marketer, I'm telling you that if you can effectively address your customers' dislikes, it can produce a powerful marketing result. So *non-smoking* is an opportunity, not a burden!

But I'm not naïve and I'm not an anti-smoking zealot. I realize that old habits die hard and many slot directors (even if they've read this far) think I'm "full of it." So I'm going to share with you my formula for using non-smoking areas as a marketing tool. If you care about your customers' peeves, if you understand that the smoking situation in society is not getting any better (what do you think all of those lawsuits are about?) and if you have some semblance of an open mind, then consider doing most, if not all off, the following:

- Considerably expand your non-smoking gaming space until it is as significant as the smoking area, just as desirable to play in and *contains all the same games and denominations as the smoking area;*

- Where possible, segregate the smoking and non-smoking areas in a design friendly way, but in a way that sends your customers the message that "the air in here is different" and not just a secondhand adjunct;

- Have your security staff enforce the non-smoking policy in the non-smoking areas;

- Buy some good quality air handling equipment for the *entire* casino;

- Start focus groups with your best customers and keep track of the number and depth of the smoking complaints, especially as you address the issue;

- "Sell" your non-smoking gaming offerings as you would anything else. Use billboards, in-house signage, advertising, newsletters, TV channels in the rooms and any other direct marketing techniques that are available;

- Stop your on-break casino employees from smoking on the casino floor (yes, some places still allow that);

- Offer more support for charities associated with "seniors" and "lungs;"

- Test your air quality regularly and honestly;

- Add some live, breathing plants on the floor; and

- Don't backpedal on this.

We've already dealt with most of gaming's stereotypes. Dealers can be friendly. We can address compulsive gambling. Casinos are good for local communities. Gamblers do win occasionally.

And casinos can have significant clean air and still be profitable. Believe it.

I am your customer (revisited)

I am your customer. I have been coming to your casino since it opened several years ago and when I think back at that time, I have to laugh. Some of my friends said you would be creating problem gamblers and breaking up families and stealing business from local companies. But heck, as I see it, all you did was create a fun night out that a *whole bunch* of my friends now enjoy.

I am your customer. Since I like your casino experience, I visit you several times per month. In fact, some time ago I joined your players club and I do like receiving some of your comps and offers — I just wish it was a little better organized. I don't understand why I have to get my table game comps "in the pit," why you can't tell me how many comp dollars are in my account, why I have to "ask" for everything I've earned and why I lose benefits and offers if I don't visit you for awhile. Heck, those small-time bus customers land and you just hand them a gift, a meal and a roll of coins — that's how I'd like it!

I am your customer. Most of your employees are pretty friendly and I've gotten to know many of them over the years. I can tell you have invested in some customer service training and it sure seems to help, but now I wish you'd do some simple stuff like having enough cage lines open on weekends and putting a few of the big bosses on the casino floor and changing some of the silly rules that only lessen my enjoyment of your casino. Do you really need to take my players club card to security when I forget and leave it in the machine?

I am your customer. I like your casino environment — it sure is exciting and not something I see every day. That is one of the reasons that I visit you. But I wish you'd fix that cold draft on the tables near the bar. And make sure those slot machines don't screech into the coffee shop while I'm enjoying my breakfast. And get some new slot stools that won't make my butt sore after only an hour of video poker. But especially, give me some non-smoking casino space that is more than a gesture (and somewhere no one currently likes to play).

I am your customer. Since I work during the week, I usually visit your casino on weekends. You sure do a heck of a business then, but sometimes I feel that you don't care about us "regulars" at these busy times. When Willie Nelson is appearing in the showroom on Saturday night, or there's 12 buses coming every weekend, or you give away a fancy car on a Sunday, all you do is make it harder for us to find our favorite game, or get a parking spot, or eat quickly so we can get back to what we came for — gambling! Why don't you do all that stuff when you really need the business?

I am your customer. I see your ads in the paper all the time … and your many fancy billboards … and your TV jingles and your cute radio commercials. God, what an advertising budget you must have! But I'll tell you a little secret. If you want me and my friends to come visit (even during the week), all you have to do is send us a personal note from one of your nice hosts or casino bosses (OK, with some little offer for us, too) and we'll beat it down to your place in a jiffy. Heck, you can even e-mail us now, we always will click on the casino's e-mail, just to see what's going on.

I am your customer. I see the good that you do for our community. I know you bought the uniforms for my kid's baseball team and the fire truck for the fire station and supported the women's shelter and give money for problem gamblers. But I know there are dozens of things you do that I must know nothing about. It may not be politically correct, but you may want to "toot your own horn" once in awhile about all this great stuff. It might help quiet some of those folks who think all you do is take people's money and don't give anything back.

Yes, I am your customer. I gamble at your tables and your slot machines. I eat at your restaurants and I use your restrooms. I park in your parking lots and sometimes I even stay in your hotel rooms. Yes, I am your customer and I am an expert. An expert about what I like about your casino. And if you asked me, I mean really *asked* me, and then really *listened*, why, then you'd be an expert on what I like about you, too.

Yes, I am your customer and the way I see it, the more you can give me what I want, the more I'll be your customer. So keep listening to me, the casinos up the road sure don't. I'd like to be your customer for a long time — and have you be the casino I call "home."

I am your employee

I am your employee. I work in your casino hotel. I am white, male and over 45 years old. I am also red, brown, yellow and black … and female … and of all working ages.

I am very new to the casino business. Or, I have worked in the casino business most of my adult life.

I am your employee. I never suspected that I would be working in a casino, but when I moved to your town, I was glad that your casino had so many different jobs available. I appreciated that many of these jobs paid a good wage and it was refreshing to see so many positions where I could earn extra money in tips.

When I found work with you, it was at one of your job fairs. The job fair was pretty interesting and I certainly didn't mind you telling me what a great employer you would be, but I would have appreciated more information on some of the stresses you find in a casino, you know, things like noise and smoke and unhappy gamblers and shift work and overtime and no child care. I know my work life can't be perfect, but I just wish I had been a little more prepared for casino life. I also think you missed a chance with your orientation to make me feel good about working for you. A tour of the property, some safety information and a list of all the prohibited employee conduct — I might have been "oriented" but I sure wasn't made welcome.

I am your employee. I work in every position at your casino. I also wear your uniforms. Don't get me wrong, I appreciate you providing my work clothes to wear. I just wish that some of the uniforms weren't so dorky looking and that others were much more functional. My coworkers tell me that they hate wearing jackets in the summer and having to wear skimpy outfits and high heels and putting on those "themed costumes" that often seem themed only to "silliness." When you are designing or choosing those uniforms, you might want to consult with the people who'll have to wear them.

I am your employee. I work according to your schedules. I know that casinos are not typical businesses, but I wonder how you manage to schedule so many of us on weekdays and so few of us on weekends when we really could use the help. I don't mind working long hours. In fact, I would love to have three or four scheduled 10 or 12 hour shifts. But it does get old going to work most nights not knowing whether I'll have to work overtime, especially because you haven't hired enough people or have several people scheduled off on the weekend.

I am your employee. I use the equipment you provide me to do my job. Actually, I "make do" with the equipment because I'm told that my department's budget doesn't allow for a new walkie-talkie for the slot floor, enough toasters in the coffee shop or a user-friendly computer terminal in the slot club booth. I certainly can get used to this equipment (or lack of it) but I really do feel sorry for our guests, as they are the ones who ultimately suffer. You might want to think about taking some of those many marketing dollars that we spend to get guests to come in our doors and spending it on the tools and systems to service them once they're here.

I am your employee. I receive your company benefits. Don't get me wrong, I know you spend a lot of money on them and I do appreciate them. It's just that I wish I had some choice in my benefits. I can't use the children's Christmas party because I don't have any kids and I don't need insurance because my wife's job covers both of us. Why couldn't I have a couple extra days off instead?

I am your employee. I work for your managers. Oh, I know that they are employees too, but sometimes you'd never know that they ever worked in my job. Oh some managers are real good — they make it a joy to be at work — but most are long on criticism and short on "attaboys." It would be nice to see them pitch in when things got busy too, and I always wondered why we see so few of the really big bosses on weekends. Isn't that when most of our customers are here?

Yes, I am your employee ... your casino/hotel employee. I am your dishwasher, your desk clerk, your dealer, your valet parker, your change attendant, your cocktail server and many others. I could work for many other companies, including other casinos, but I have chosen to work for you. The best of us aren't too demanding. In fact, our needs are simple. Be nice to me, treat me with respect and show me you care.

And I will be your casino employee for a long time.

More pet peeves

I'm not a whiner. I'm really not.

But OK, maybe I am critical … maybe even *too* critical. But what the hell, someone needs to point this stuff out.

A while back, I wrote a column on "My Pet Peeves" and I railed away against that stuff in the casino world that personally ticks me off. You know, stuff like arrogant craps dealers and lines outside of half-empty restaurants and being told I have to cash out my coins *someplace else* and having to *ask* for comps.

You know, that kind of stuff.

Well you know what? It was very therapeutic to unload my pet peeves on you, my unwary readers. Well OK, one reader *did* want to incessantly argue about how *unfair* I was toward craps dealers.

But anyway, I did feel better after that column so in the past year I've been looking for even more pet peeves in our wonderful world of casinos.

They weren't too hard to find.

More of my pet peeves:

It's not my station — Hey, Ms. Food and Beverage Director, didn't you realize that all of your cocktail servers dress alike? Didn't you realize that all of your food servers dress alike? I realize I'm just a poor dumb customer slob, but you know what? Their name is *server*, not *non-server*. So why can't they serve me? Union issues? Baloney. Short staff? Hire more people. Don't know how to manage it? Take a course on it. The truth is, Ms. Culinary Office Jockey, that you don't care enough about my experience to figure out how *all* of your servers could actually "serve" me. I know it's possible. Have you checked out how Bubba Gump's Restaurants does it? You should.

You'll have to get your table game comps from the pit — You know, I'm really sorry that I'm a table game player and that I create all of these problems for your high falutin' tracking system. But you know what Mr. High Paid Casino Marketing Executive? I never asked for any player reward system (Oh, I won't turn down your stupid "incentives" even if I would still play without them). Don't you think if I go to your players club that I should be able to get a "player's" comp, especially after you've made me go beg for it? At the very least you might put up a goddamn sign saying, "Table Game Players Not Welcome Here!"

The security "cop" — Now, I'll be honest, I do feel secure in your casino, Mr. Chief of Security. But hey, it's supposed to be "casino entertainment." I think that means we're supposed to be having *fun*. So why the uniforms straight out of the LAPD? Why the suspicious scowls when I come in your main entrance? Why the grudging responses when I ask where the restroom is? I'll tell you why, Mr. Battalion Chief. You've trained great cops but lousy customer servants.

3:00 p.m. check-in — Ms. Hotel Vice President, I know it's really inconvenient for you when I check in at 10:00 a.m., but do you know how goddamn inconvenient it is *for me* to come back in five hours to check in??? And then get kicked out of my room because of your wonderfully restrictive 11:00 a.m. check-out time??! Can't you do better than this???

The coupon criminal cue — Hey, Mr. Grand Poobah of Marketing, if you are going to put out a coupon to your customers, you might try telling your frontline operations staff about it. It's bad enough having your employees not know what the hell the coupon is for, but even worse is when I get treated like a criminal just for having it. May I suggest you redeem one of your own coupons one day, so that you can see the hoops you make *me* jump through?

Turtle-like hopper fills — Ms. Slot Director, let me explain something to you. When my slot machine runs out of money, it's when it is in the process of either paying me or cashing me out. Now those are two of my very best slot experiences — getting paid and getting cashed out! That is, until I'm stuck to my chair waiting for your overworked, underpaid staff to get to me. Here's my free slot marketing plan for you, Ms. Cost Conscious — get some new equipment, change your customer unfriendly regulations and hire a few more people. Maybe then you can have your profit bandits out of commission for less than 15 minutes at a time.

Employee-only windows — Hey, Mr. Cage Manager, I see them. You all do it — *employee-only windows*. Sure I know what you're doing. You're trying to make sure that your employees can serve your customers quickly. But last I knew *I* was your customer. Sorry, just a pet peeve I guess.

A call for a new casino host model

Several years ago, Disney got into the timeshare business. It took a look at the then standard time share sales model and decided it was a high-pressure, almost sleazy way of selling vacations. So it changed the model, totally banned all high-pressure sales techniques and instituted simple, fun features to the selling process, such as serving ice cream instead of B.S. to potential buyers.

When it first came into being, Saturn took a look at the automobile sales model and decided it was a high-pressure, almost sleazy way of selling cars. So Saturn changed the model, introduced no-haggle pricing and started focusing on building relationships instead of churning car sales. And now Saturn's customers are the most loyal of all customers in the auto business.

It's time that someone built a new model for the whole casino host system.

I realize that for some of you who work for small casinos, these remarks will not make much sense, for you probably do not even employ casino hosts.

I also realize that among the rest of you that have a host system, it likely includes many diligent, hard-working employees that are among the best *people* people on your property.

Still, there are some fundamental, deep flaws in the casino host system and it's time someone changed the model. It may not be as sleazy as most timeshare sales, but at the very least, the casino host system is morally suspect and of questionable long-term business value.

Pretty harsh assessment, I realize. Let me make my point.

Casino hosts have the sometimes enviable job of locating and then bonding with premium casino customers. Whether they are paid $30,000 at a remote tribal casino or $200,000 at a fancy Las Vegas Strip property, their jobs are the same: *Find good casino customers and get them to visit as often and as exclusively (to the host's casino) as possible.*

A noble goal, sure. But from my experience, here's what's wrong with casino host models across North America:

Lack of clear definition of who "owns" the casino customers — Sure casino hosts sign confidentiality agreements when they begin employment. But then how are so many hosts able to run to work for a competitor, making thousands of dollars more, usually carrying with them a long list of purloined gamblers?

System eventually corrupts — The host system gives a few casino employees "the keys to the city" and allows them to bestow gifts, comps and favors upon select customers, usually in a very legitimate fashion. However, many of these grateful customers will attempt to bestow gifts, cash and favors upon their favorite hosts. This corrupts the system and many hosts will be unable to resist the temptation of accepting these tokens of appreciation, which usually run against company policy.

The split table game and slot host departments — Believe it or not, many casinos still have one set of hosts for table games and another for slots. This causes inefficiency and customer unfriendly job descriptions.

Lack of teamwork — The current host model pushes casino hosts to be "independent contractors" instead of cooperative members of a high powered, hosting team.

Too much focus on existing customers — Although most hosts are responsible for finding "new" customers, many hosts fall victim to spending most of their time with their long-time loyal customers. It's easier, probably more personally profitable for the host and allows them to build some substance to "their" player list.

Lack of training — Casino hosts usually learn from each other so the system inbreeds itself. But where will a new host learn ethics, sales skills, how to approach a new customer, fundamental principles of life-time player worth, teamwork, dealing with demanding customers and a variety of other critically important topics?

Short-term mindset — Casino hosts usually focus on *now*, getting customers to come in on the next offer or for the next event. There are no strategies to be seen for maximizing long-term customer value.

No internal flow of good people — When it's time to hire a host, casinos usually look to the "breed of hosts," usually at their competitors. This ignores super-friendly and high-potential people at their own casino, missing a chance to build solid career paths and develop strong employee loyalty. It also further perpetuates the sleazy, list-brokering environment in casinos.

No commission-based pay system — The casino host position is the one casino job closest to a *pure sales job*. Yet rarely is there even a commission structure for hosts or it's an inconsequential component of the overall host pay scale.

So what would I do with this flawed host model? Simple, scrap it and start over. Then I'd build a new model — one with integrity, accountability and teamwork.

I know it must be possible.

Building customer service standards in *your* department

To improve customer service at your Indian casino, it is important to have customer service standards for all positions in your department. These standards must be written documents and they must possess the following qualities:

- They must *matter* to the customers whom they are designed to serve;

- They must be *simple* to understand;

- They must be *realistic* to the position for which they are written;

- They must be *clear* and *tangible*;

- They must be *achievable* by the employees in the positions for which they were written;

- They must be *consistent* with the service standards within the department and at the property; and

- They must be *measurable*, even if it is only by a "yes" or "no" response.

Within the gaming industry, casino customer service standards for employees run the gamut from "non-existent" to "detailed and extensive." One company goes so far as to break down each job into all of its particular aspects and then establishes concrete corresponding behaviors. But more common are the casino companies that have no standards or loosely defined, loosely applied service standards.

Developing and utilizing clear and meaningful customer service standards is one of your greatest opportunities to positively impact your casino guests' experience and your casino company's bottom line.

Start by thinking like a customer:

Let's use the example of the casino dealer position. We could begin to develop customer service standards for this position by getting input from dealers, pit supervisors, training specialists, table games managers and a host of other individuals. But ultimately the only opinion that matters is the opinion of the table games customer. In a customer-focused Indian gaming company, should it be any other way?

Know what your customer wants:

In our table games example, to develop effective customer service standards, you must know what your customers want in their table game service. If you do not know, you will need to find out. And the best way to find out is to *ask your customer*.

This can be done in a variety of ways:

- Informally, through a dedicated series of casual discussions with table games customers;

- Formally, through scientific techniques like focus groups and customer surveys;

- Indirectly, through conversations with table games employees;

- Experientially, by becoming a customer and finding out what matters to you; and

- Any combination of the above.

Do not limit your standards to smiles:

There is often a tendency to define service standards around how friendly you want your employees to act and whether or not they say specific, customer-friendly phrases ("Good Luck," "Hello," "Thank You," etc.). While these are certainly important, do not forget the other things that are important to a customer. In our table games example, customers might value a game that moves at the right speed, error-free dealing and concern for the quality of their experience (cocktails, player rating, suggestions for dining or entertainment, etc.). If your customer service standards are limited to *smile* and *greet the guest*, you will have missed the chance to define other meaningful service behaviors.

Use specific time and quantity standards whenever possible:

Casino guests do not usually know exactly how long certain transactions take between themselves and your employees. They only know when it *takes too long*. Likewise, they have no idea that an experienced blackjack dealer should easily deal 400 hands per hour, they only know when the game *moves too slow or too fast.*

In writing your standards however, you should always try to include the exact times and quantities that you expect from your employees in various situations (e.g. three minutes to answer a slot guest call for assistance, five minutes to handle one credit application transaction, etc.). Of course, individual circumstances vary greatly, especially when it is busy, but at least you will have a *concrete* number to manage against. If your service evaluations continually show that a five-minute transaction time is never met, for instance, then either the standard is too high, you need more staff (or better-trained staff) or there may be coordination issues with other departments.

If the goal is quick service, define how quick!

Understand your employees' service capabilities:

If customer service is a new concept for your Indian gaming employees, or if your workforce contains many new or unskilled people, you do not want your customer service standards to be complex, extensive or too demanding. As your employees accept and are able to master an achievable set of customer service standards you will be able to easily add to those standards.

Tie into your employee evaluations:

If you are going to have customer service standards, they should logically be a part of your employee evaluations. If you do not *inspect* what you *expect*, in a common language that looks the same in the "standards" text as it does in the "evaluation" text, you will not get the needed buy-in from your employees that customer service standards are important. And if you do not appropriately *reward* and *discipline* according to how those standards are being met, you will have not given your employees any real reason to follow and exceed your customer service standards, other than perhaps the fear of losing their job.

Be flexible in application:

Customer service standards can often look the same to every employee. But all employees are different and have different skills. Some employees are shyer than others. Some cultures are more reserved than others and "being friendly" may not include laughing and joking with customers. Your customer service standards, or at least your evaluation of your employees' ability to follow them, should recognize these differences.

Train to your standards:

In our dealer example, if you want your employees to welcome customers to the game and wish them good luck, you must show them how you want that to happen in the table games area. You must have the training necessary to support that desired service behavior. Formal service training, on the job training, everyday coaching by supervisors — all of these tools must be utilized vigorously and often for your standards to have real value.

If you want to improve customer service in your department at your Indian casino, you need to have clear but flexible standards, customer listening posts, accountability and rewards. Sounds simple, doesn't it? Well, what are you waiting for? The welfare of your department, and maybe even your tribe, depends on it.

'Happy Birthday' — casino style

It was a spur of the moment thing. The free room night offer came as a birthday gift from Harrah's, and when I realized that I was going to be in town for my birthday, it seemed like a perfect time for my wife and I to take one of those very special getaways, a one night mini-vacation right in our very own town.

And while I certainly do not want to bore you with "a look through the family photo album," I do think that my birthday experiences might just have a few lessons for your Native American casino, especially as it relates to how you help your casino customers celebrate.

We pulled into valet parking at the Harrah's Hotel Casino entrance. The attendant was there within 15 seconds, warmly greeted me, asked for my name (and used it in the transaction) and wished us a "great time" at Harrah's. We strolled into the hotel registration area and noticed a special, line-free "Platinum Card Holders" check-in desk. The whole check-in process, even with my special direct mail offer, took less than 90 seconds and was friendly and efficient. We were offered help with our bags and given directions to the proper hotel tower.

My birthday vacation was off to a great start!

My wife had made reservations for a nice, quiet dinner at the Harrah's Steakhouse, so that left us a couple of hours to go have some fun. We decided to walk two blocks to a brand new casino that had been open for a few months and where I had played previously. The small casino had a nice ambiance (although it was already rumored to be experiencing financial difficulties) and my wife and I especially liked its downstairs wine cellar bar and its unique selection of various "wine flights." A great place to start my birthday celebration!

I knew from my previous play at "Casino X" that I certainly had accumulated some "comp dollars" and as I bought into the craps game, I asked the floor person there how much credit for the wine bar I might be able to use.

"You have $70 of comp dollars," he told me, after looking in his computer.

"Great," I said. "Please make me out a comp ticket for the wine bar."

He returned with a comp ticket for $25.

"Well, I have my wife with me and the wine flights we like cost $25 each, so could you give me the whole $70 or at least another $25 comp?" I asked.

"We don't normally do comps for the wine bar, but I'll see what I can do," the floor person promised.

He returned about 10 minutes later with another $25 "coupon" for the wine cellar. The coupon was part of a hotel "Sweetheart Getaway" package and could be used for the wine cellar.

"This will work just fine," he said. "We don't like to give comps for the wine cellar because you never know how much a person might spend down there."

I didn't say anything to him, but I was getting hot. I had $70 in credit coming, and they gave me $25. I had to *ask* for more, then I received a *coupon* instead of the normal comp slip. I had to wait for an answer. I had to hear about their internal issues.

It was obvious to me that I was dealing with a casino trying to save a few bucks on their complimentary expenses, a casino which a premium player would have trouble doing business with. But I was not going to let it spoil my birthday!

My wife and I went downstairs to the wine bar. The $25 coupon I was given had expired. The bartender treated us with some suspicion, but at least called over her supervisor, the wine steward, to handle the situation. I expected my horror story at "Casino X" to continue.

Thankfully, the sommelier graciously accepted the expired coupon. He then proceeded to personally recommend a customized wine flight for us to enjoy, telling us about "bouquets" and other wine "stuff." We even bought a bottle that we especially liked.

But the wine steward's "recovery" couldn't overcome our bad casino experience. Even though, after wine, my wife and I had some time to gamble before dinner, we chose to go back to Harrah's to play. "Casino X" would get no more of our business.

Harrah's acted like they knew it was my birthday, even though I didn't tell them. The craps dealer welcomed me and used my name, which he gleaned from my player's card. The table games supervisor was gracious and comped a portion of my dinner, even though he didn't have to. The maitre d' at the steakhouse allowed us to bring in our own bottle of wine to the restaurant with no corkage fee. He gave us a premium table and made both dinner and drink recommendations. The food was great and the service was great. It was a perfect birthday dinner, a winning gaming experience and a wonderful weekend getaway, thanks to Harrah's and its people.

I think the moral of my birthday story is that many times guests come to your Indian casino to celebrate — a birthday, an anniversary, heck, even a night out. When they do, will their experience be more like my Harrah's visit, or my torture at "Casino X?"

Help your guests celebrate and they won't mind at all spending their dollars at your Indian casino.

My pet peeves (revisited)

I have written several times about the things that personally tick me off at casinos — not only tribal casinos, but *all* casinos. You see, I gamble everywhere I go in the gaming world, so I am qualified to speak on these matters. After all, I am your customer.

Now the same things that upset most of your customers are not the same things that irritate me. Well, some of them are, but mostly it's different stuff, maybe a function of being around casinos for 30 years.

What upsets the majority of your customers is easy, and I have heard it time and time again in focus groups I have conducted or witnessed at both tribal and non-tribal casinos. Tight machines, smoke, long lines and waits, employees who don't have answers or are rude, being taken for granted — there, that's pretty much it. So why aren't you doing something about these things?

But the things that annoy me are different. I've written about some of them: long lines at restaurants when whole restaurant sections are closed; having to "ask" for comps; jackpot bell assault weapons; 3:00 p.m. check-ins; being treated like a criminal (or a "flea") for trying to use one of *your* coupons — you know, stuff like that. And you know what? It is very therapeutic to get this stuff off my chest. So here are some more pet peeves, or as I like to say:

Casino stuff that drives me crazy
(My editor says it is a short drive):

Scolding signs — You know, by now I realize that you can throw me out of your tribal casino for any reason you wish. I know I can't bring drugs, firearms or alcohol into the casino. I almost know the "Rules of Prohibited Conduct" by heart. So why are the first things I so often see at your entrances, threatening signs? Wouldn't a sign saying, "Welcome, have fun!" be more appropriate for a "gaming entertainment" center??? It would at least make passing the security guard gauntlet at the front a little less daunting.

Coinless and "thrill-less" — I actually do like your new coinless machines. My eardrums like them. I like not having to wait for those fills and most jackpot payoffs. And I really like not having my hands get dirty or having to lug those heavy buckets of coins over to the cashier to cash out. But you know what, some of the thrill is gone. I had a royal flush the other day and nothing happened … *nothing*. The credits racked up and the game was ready for the next spin. Nobody came. I mean, I had to yell at my neighbor three stools over so he could see how lucky I'd been. So find a way to put some of the thrill back, I don't know how, just do it!

Whining employees — Hey, Ms. HR Director, I know it's not easy (I have my own business with employees, too), but can't you stop some of that employee "whining?" At least all that whining in front of us customers? You know, I really don't care that it's their second straight day of overtime, or that they think your new casino promotion is stupid, or even that all of the good jobs are going to Native Americans (hey, isn't that the idea?!). I just don't want to hear it; I want to escape all that stuff. That's why I come to the casino!

Those nasty bus customers — They are probably very nice people, but hey Mr. Marketing Director, have you ever been in the casino when two or three busses full of customers land at once? They clog your players club, they flood your restaurant, but worst of all, dammit, they hog my favorite machines, playing one coin at a time! When I see a bus at the casino now, I just turn around and go home. And you know what else? I see the goodies those bus customers get — free meals, giveaway items, rolls of coins. Hey, what about me??? Don't you want to give your best goodies to your best customers?

Paper towels in restrooms — You do a great job of keeping the restrooms clean, Mr. Facilities Director, I really mean that. And this peeve will probably seem petty. But I don't care. How do you manage to get the paper towel dispensers so far from the sinks? It never fails. Is someone plotting this? I mean, I get more water on your restroom floor than I do on the paper towel, by the time I find it. Oh well, one good "slip and fall" claim will probably fix that.

Valet parking — I don't know, but isn't valet parking the first and last point of contact with your Indian casino customers? I love the convenience and service upon arrival is pretty quick, but after coming to your place twice a week for two years, shouldn't someone know my name by now? And why does it take so long to get my car when I want to leave? Is it a conspiracy to get me to stay? Looks like poor staffing to me. And tell those young whippersnapper valet parkers when they return my car that I don't want my radio dial changed to a punk rock or Spanish music station! And couldn't they open my door for me??? I mean, what would happen if I *didn't* tip them?

So there you have it, Mr. General Manager or Madame Tribal Chairperson — my pet peeves. And I realize I'm just some poor customer slob, but I want you to know that this customer slob spent $8,000 at your tribal casino last year … $100 at a whack, like clockwork. I just thought you'd like to know. I *like* your Indian casino and I *love* what it does for your people. But too many pet peeves and I'm going somewhere where they care about making me happy. Believe it.

Selling the casino

For a long time, I have felt that our industry does a poor job of selling the casino experience. Oh sure, casinos spend a ton of money on advertising, direct mail, promotional giveaways, signage and numerous other things that are designed to entice casino players into our facilities. That is not the selling to which I am referring.

The "selling of the casino" that I want to discuss involves all of those interactions where casino employees have the opportunity to "sell" to casino customers at your tribal casino. You know, where the greeter at the front door (security officer or not!) suggests to arriving guests that they try the buffet … where a dealer mentions to a player at the 21 table that the progressive video poker jackpot at the bar is exceptionally high … where the valet parker, noting an out of state license plate, asks an arriving guest if they are staying at the casino's hotel that evening and if they are aware of the midweek room discount. You know, *that* kind of selling.

And having visited hundreds of casinos and had literally thousands of employee interactions at these gaming facilities, I can tell you that almost *none* of this type of selling is taking place — where employees attempt to show customers how to spend more money at the casino facility. And herein lies a tremendous opportunity for your Indian casino.

I know what you are thinking. "Heck, it's hard enough getting most employees just to do their jobs and smile, and now you want us to turn them into salespeople???" Well, yes, actually. And why not? Shouldn't every employee at your tribal casino be knowledgeable about the entire operation and proud to suggest ways for customers to have more fun and get more value from your casino entertainment?

Of course they should!!!

Now, I am not naïve. I do understand that if you tell your security officers that you want them to be salespersons for the buffet that they'll probably give you that same look you get when you inform them that you need them to work six days next week (and remember, they may have a gun!).

Well hey, I never said that it would be easy!

But rather than focus on the barriers to getting your casino employees to be salespeople, let's talk about some essential tactics and principles for how you can make this happen. Remember, turning your casino employees into salespeople has *millions* of potential dollars of revenue for your casino operation. Do you realize the impact that McDonald's had on its bottom line just by getting (mostly minimum wage) employees to ask, "Would you like fries with that?"

So get those employees selling your Indian gaming experience. And here's how:

Write sales roles into all job descriptions — If you want food servers to "sell" desserts by bringing out a tray of yummy looking sugar items, *then make that their job!*

Hire the right people — I know, I know, this is easier said than done, but if you look for enthusiasm, smiles and communication ability in potential employees, you'll be that much closer to having real *sales* people.

Train, train, train — Except for one unique instance, I have not seen any examples of sales training taking place in the casino environment. Oh sure, some room reservationists (check out the ones at Harrah's Rincon) are trained to upsell rooms and most waiters will have (finally) been trained to ask diners if they want to see a wine list, but beyond that, *nothing.*

Employee samples — If you want them to sell it, let them touch it, taste it, experience it! Every one of your employees should personally be allowed to sample everything you have to offer — food, rooms, promotions — everything! Yes, there is a price tag and your CFO will squirm when you tell her you want to give away 1,000 buffet meals to employees so they "know what you're selling," but your employees can't sell what they don't know. Unless, of course, you are ashamed of the quality of your buffet.

Inspect and reward — So how do you know your employees are now selling your casino? Well, your managers are looking for it; they are praising it when it occurs and counseling when it doesn't. And for god sakes, put a few reward bucks behind it! What is it worth to you to have a food server sell 1,000 bottles of wine in a year??? Share the success. Why do you think salespeople always work on commission anyway?

Getting your tribal casino employees to sell all aspects of your gaming experience is one of the most powerful things you can do and it doesn't take even one additional employee. Unless of course you want to create the position of "Vice President of Sales." Now there's a concept!

How to listen to your customers

I have met very few people in the gaming industry who don't believe in the importance of listening to their gaming customers. In fact, I believe that my company's simple mantra of "Find Out What Your Customers Want and Give It To Them" has been at the heart of our success because it reverberates with the beliefs of most casino executives on the value of these listening posts. And yet too few casinos religiously, effectively and comprehensively monitor feedback from their casino customers, especially their *best* casino customers.

So what's going on here? Why the disconnect???

Well, I believe this is a situation where the "spirit is willing, but the flesh is weak." Most casinos want to listen to their customers, try to listen to their customers and might even believe they *do* listen to their customers. But from my experience, all of that "goo" (budgets, meetings, reports, employee issues, etc., etc., etc.) gets squarely in the way of really listening to our customers. It's kind of like listening to our car radio when driving out in the country. We'd like to hear the song, but the static from the radio is too high!

So I have given this great thought and I have analyzed the casinos that do a pretty good job of gathering and effectively using their guests' feedback. So I'd like to share my thoughts with you now. I believe it's pretty important stuff.

Important principles for listening to your customers:

Consistency is more important than any single tactic — Whether you are listening to your customers through organized focus groups, exit surveys, customer advisory boards or just good old-fashioned "one on ones" on the casino floor, it is more important that you keep doing it on a regular basis than using any one specific magic listening bullet.

A comment card program does not qualify as a listening program — Comment cards, no matter how well marketed or used, tend to attract participation from either your *very happy* or your *very upset* customers. It is hard to make important, strategic business decisions by listening to the "fringes."

The GM should dedicate time to listening to live, breathing casino customers — Whether it's just walking the casino floor or hanging out during the VIP event or the promotional drawing, the GM needs to hear from *real* casino customers. He or she will get a definite earful. And it will put real meaning into those charts or numbers on "guest satisfaction" that come across the cherry wood desk.

Some customers opinions count more than others — Sure, you care about keeping your "two-bit" customers and your buffet-goers happy, but let's face it. The 80/20 rule applies and the opinions of your best customers count more than others. So listen mostly to your best customers.

Listen hard to what your customers are really saying — I have never been to a casino where its best customers *did not* say "the slot machines have gotten tighter since the casino first opened." This is the natural result of playing "negative expectation" games over time. But that doesn't mean you automatically go out and loosen your slot hold percentage by 1 percent (a huge expense!). Maybe it means they want more nickel machines, or machines with a higher "hit frequency" or just want to feel like a winner when they do win (congratulations, celebrations, "way to go," etc.). So listen hard!

Have ALL of your casino's executives listen to your customers — When I last worked for a casino property, one of the best exercises we did was to have all of our senior executives call good customers who hadn't visited in the past year (and find out why). Oh sure, several execs hated the exercise, but the information we gained was truly eye-opening. So make sure even the CFO gets piped in to your customers!

Listen to your employees too! — Sometimes we think it is just about the *customer* customer. But employees are customers, too. And not only are they piped in to what customers are saying, but these employees are critical to the success of your tribal casino, often having ideas and suggestions worth thousands or even millions of dollars!

Now that you're listening, act on the information — Remember, the deal is to find out what your customers (and employees) want so that you can give it to them. So when they tell you to fix the restrooms, do it!

Take these principles to heart when listening to your customers at your tribal casino. You may just find that they have no reason to go to the casino down the street because "Hey, they never listen to me!"

Stories

The story of the "Pull Me More" group

The following story represents a little known and probably little cared about piece of gaming industry history. The people in the story have gone their separate ways — one has died — and even they themselves might think little about what they contributed in the few short months that they came together. I share that story now, for what it can teach us today about the power of innovation and how much potential resides deep in every single casino employee that toils in our industry.

The time was 1992 and I was the casino marketing manager at the Harrah's property on the Las Vegas Strip, which was undergoing a name change, becoming Harrah's Las Vegas and shedding the name Holiday Casino. My mentor had recently departed for another, bigger job in Las Vegas and I was left alone to fend for myself in the heady casino marketing world that he had created. I had recently finished an "inquisition" into the value of our free spending department and if I should be the one to continue to lead it.

Well I survived that inquisition, mainly because my new boss was fair minded, needed people who could make things happen and recognized that I had busted my tail for the past five years in an environment that questioned every casino marketing activity that we executed.

While my new vice president of casino operations kept me on "his team," he also made it clear that our singular focus was to be on driving slot business. He wanted me to do anything I could to achieve that goal and mentioned that occasionally he would come to me with a strategic slot issue and ask me to propose solutions.

It didn't take long for him to bring me the first dilemma. He walked me over to an area of the slot floor that was wedged between the coffee shop and the hotel lobby — little wonder that slot revenues here were a fraction of the "house average." He asked me to come up with a creative concept that would attract players to this area instead of repel them.

Now I'm a fairly creative guy and I instantly thought of several concepts that I thought had value. But I was also *not* a slot player and I had no idea if these "machine people" would care two hoots about any new "slot innovation" I was trying to bring them. So I decided to ask for help. No, not from a consultant, but from our employees.

I didn't care if this help came from frontline employees or managers. I didn't care in what department they worked or on what shift. I looked only for people who seemed pretty intelligent and opinionated, and who regularly played slots themselves in several casinos in the Las Vegas area. So I approached employees that I knew who fit these criteria and asked other employees to recommend co-workers as well. And this is what I ended up with for our "Creative Slot Committee:" an administrative assistant who had 16 local casinos' players club cards; a tournament coordinator who played video poker as her sole hobby; a slot change person with a gift of gab who not only played slots herself, but bantered routinely with other players whenever she played; and a slot supervisor who was known as a "complainer," but whose complaints always seemed to be valid and represented real customer concerns.

I appointed myself as the facilitator for these new slot innovators and we arranged to meet every week for two hours to discuss revenue-generating slot ideas. In the first meeting, the group decided it should have a name and since the goal was increased slot play, they called themselves The Pull Me More Group. Remember, this was still the era where players almost always pulled the slot handle instead of hit the slot spin button. So the Pull Me Mores were born.

And in that first meeting, I brought up that gnarly slot area between the hotel and the restaurant where no one liked to play. I watched the group argue, challenge each other, laugh, come up with some absolutely crazy ideas and make me wonder if we would ever produce anything useful. But then the talk turned to slot areas where *they* liked to play and to unique slot environments that they had seen in and around Las Vegas. And in three weeks, the Pull Me Mores recommended that this underperforming slot area be transformed into "Hitters," a sports-themed slot area with not only sports memorabilia on the wall, but also the pictures, signatures and testimonials of all the slot players who "hit" jackpots in this slot zone.

In subsequent weeks, the Pull Me Mores designed the gaming industry's first complete slot celebration process, decided what to do with the progressive slot jackpot amounts of four slot games which were being taken off the floor (and whose progressive amounts had to *somehow* be distributed to players) and addressed other sundry slot promotion issues. I don't remember why the group eventually stopped meeting. Perhaps the VP stopped issuing us challenges; perhaps I dropped the ball; perhaps it was what inevitably happens when you tap into the power of your employees and don't continue to tap hard enough or give them enough reason to continue to give us the discretionary value of their wisdom and creativity.

Whatever the reason, I do know that the Pull Me More Group had great value for the casino, the group participants loved it and the quantity and quality of the creative results we generated were far greater than anything any of us could have accomplished alone. And that's when I learned that there is so much more that good people are capable of doing if you can get over that wall called their "job description." You should try it some time.

A marketing miracle

Well, it may not have been a miracle, but it certainly is one of the best casino business "turnaround" stories that I have ever heard about and I think it contains great lessons for your own casino or your own company.

Here's the story.

The Imperial Palace in Mississippi was built on the "Back Bay" near Biloxi, Miss. around the turn of the century by the late Ralph Engelstad, owner of the Imperial Palace in Las Vegas. It was built in the image and likeness of the Vegas IP, a design style that might fairly be called an "industrial strength Asian theme."

The Imperial Palace Mississippi struggled immediately after opening. It had an inferior location a couple of miles off the Biloxi Gulf Coast beachfront, where significant competitors Grand Casino, Casino Magic, Isle of Capri and Beau Rivage (among others) were located. It had a bland, stark facility with few amenities. Its food product paled in comparison to other nearby casinos. It couldn't attract superior employees and those that did sign up to work at the Imperial Palace Mississippi settled into it being "just another job." The irascible owner insisted on running the property like it was in Las Vegas and his formula for "cheap rooms, cheap customers" soon made the Imperial Palace the tacky choice in the market.

Then Ralph Engelstad died. The executors of his estate were faced with the choice of selling this underperforming casino asset or somehow, some way, finding a miracle worker to turn it around.

Enter Jon Lucas.

Jon was a well-respected, senior gaming operator from Caesars Entertainment, who became available as a result of the Harrah's buyout of Caesars. Approached by the Imperial Palace executors, Jon did what any savvy gaming executive would do — he went to experience the Imperial Palace as a customer. It was not a pretty picture and Jon minced no words in reporting back bluntly to the estate managers. Furthermore, he told them the property needed a lot of money to be competitive and if they were not prepared to make that commitment then he was not the guy to help them.

To their credit, the estate executors made that commitment and used Jon Lucas to make the Imperial Palace imperial for the first time. He

108

began the long and arduous process of analyzing the customer base and the marketing, cleaning up the place, putting his senior team together and tackling the issue of the poor food product.

And then Katrina hit the Gulf Coast.

No one was spared from Katrina including the Imperial Palace. But its Back Bay location, a few precious miles away from the Gulf, and its sturdy building, now a benefit rather than just a bland design, spared the Imperial Palace from the terrible fate of the other Biloxi/Gulfport casinos. They were all destroyed.

The Imperial Palace now had a huge competitive advantage and could have exploited that to open quickly and make as much money as possible in a short-term monopoly environment in the Gulf Coast. But Jon Lucas had a vision and a plan.

He allowed the Imperial Palace to be used first as a hotel for relief workers dealing with the Katrina devastation. He sought to build bridges with the community which desperately needed assistance and with which the Imperial Palace had had a previous strained relationship. He started remodeling the hotel rooms in preparation for a reopening. He added restaurants. He hired new managers and new employees (who were happy to have a place to work) from the more service-oriented casinos in the area while retaining as many original Imperial Palace employees as he could. Jon and his team changed not only a building, but an entire culture, reflected aptly in its new name, "the IP Casino Resort Spa." It reopened just before Christmas of 2005, not even four months after Katrina.

And today? Well, I stayed at the IP recently. The rooms were well appointed and comfortable. The food was excellent and the restaurant "32" (on the 32nd floor) was remarkable. The spa was outstanding and the casino was busy (and I enjoyed the 20X odds on craps). There were lounges and nightclubs and Starbucks and gift shops. The entire IP transformation was stunning (I had been to the old Imperial Palace pre-Katrina).

I ran into Jon Lucas and asked him his secret for his remarkable IP success, which is holding even as Harrah's, MGM Mirage and Isle of Capri rebuild their Gulf Coast businesses. And he boiled it down to this:

- Broaden the amenities to attract a broader customer base with more money to spend;

- Create an excellent food product;

- Get your hands around the marketing and target the right customers;

- Dramatically improve customer service and hire service-oriented employees;

- Have a management team that buys into your vision and executes the plan; and

- Get meaningfully involved in the community and give back in a meaningful way.

"Worst to First" — as simple as that. Congratulations, Jon Lucas and the entire IP team. It may not be a marketing miracle, but it's pretty damn close.

The "Southwest Airlines Casino"

I travel a lot in my consulting work, so I have the dubious pleasure of flying on a lot of airplanes. After 9/11 and for many months thereafter, it was a royal hassle to fly, but for whatever reason (maybe you just get used to the snarls), it seems to at least be manageable again. And I actually believe airline service has improved — it has gone from awful to poor.

I was thinking about this as my plane was on the tarmac after landing on time (!) in Miami. The pilot came on the speaker saying that it would be "just a few minutes" until we got to the gate as another plane was exiting it. Thirty minutes later (with no further explanation), I exited the plane, now with a tight connection for a flight leaving from the other end of the terminal. On the plane they had (nicely, I thought) told us our connecting information and gate numbers. Heck, you know the rest of the story — gate change, wild goose chase through the terminal, almost miss my flight.

This would never happen on Southwest Airlines. At Southwest, service is great, systems are simple and things actually work! I shudder to think of my rating for airline service without the attentiveness of Southwest.

From Reno, I fly Southwest probably 80 percent to 90 percent of the time (mostly because Southwest has kicked every other airline's butt in that market). Between those hundreds of Southwest flights and the thousands of Southwest employees I've encountered, plus the several books I've read about Southwest (I recommend "Nuts!" and "The Southwest Airlines Way"), I feel somewhat of an expert on the Southwest formula. And boy, could casinos learn a thing or two from it! Here's why I think SWA is so successful and what I think the corresponding application is for the casino industry:

1. Low prices, no frills — Southwest has everyday low prices and simple point-to-point, (mostly) short haul air service. It doesn't gum it up with fancy, first-class options, or long hauls on huge planes to exotic locations or in-flight food service.

Casinos, hello? Your customers without fail say they also want a simple gaming experience with good time on device, a reasonable chance to win and some basic feeling of value for their discretionary entertainment dollar. But noooooo ... we give them double points and car give-aways and coupons and entertainment on Saturdays. Somehow I think the Southwest Airlines Casino would be a lot simpler.

2. Relational competence — That's what Southwest calls it and it means that its employees are hired and trained in *working together.* That's why Southwest flight attendants clean the flight cabin (in minutes, usually while passengers deplane), why pilots act as greeters, why gate agents and flight crews can execute 10-minute boardings and 20-minute flight turnarounds.

In the Southwest Airlines Casino, you'd see pit and slot employees work together (heaven forbid!) for the benefit of the *gaming* guest. You'd see an employee from another department get a drink for a thirsty guest without worry of a union grievance. You'd see the GM as a visible greeter, because hey, he flies this casino plane!

3. Fun — I can't tell you the number of times Southwest has made me smile (besides its warm, friendly ads). Whether it's the irreverent safety instructions, or being serenaded in song by a flight attendant upon landing or watching a six-year-old Southwest passenger help hand out bags of nuts — flying Southwest is just plain fun!

And those would be the hallmarks of the Southwest Airlines Casino — playfulness, humor, lively interactions. No more clueless dealers, or slot employees going through the motions or cage employees with no personality. No, at the Southwest Airlines Casino, employees understand they are on stage and the customer came for short-haul entertainment!

4. Easy to do business with — If you are ever at an airport where Southwest flies, watch the movement of their check-in lines at the ticket counter. It probably processes passengers twice as fast as other airlines. This isn't because its employees are administrative wizards, but because all of Southwest's systems support rapid passenger processing. It has online check-in, numerous airport check-in kiosks and a host of other technology and system solutions to move passengers efficiently.

In the Southwest Airlines Casino, key points of contact would be geared around moving gaming guests (especially VIPs) through the numerous, everyday casino transactions. There would be redemption kiosks, online inquiry and point redemption capabilities for players club transactions and simple, friendly employee interactions with a minimum of hassles. No more "Take this to the cage" or "Fill out this application" or

"Table game chip transactions are at another window." No, the Southwest Airlines Casino would recognize that being "easy to do business with" is a great marketing tool itself and minimizes those dreaded lines that casino managers and casino guests both detest.

5. *Easy to use, meaningful rewards* — Southwest Airlines' frequent flyer program, Rapid Rewards, is simple to understand, easy to use and has meaningful benefits. Fly eight roundtrips and earn a free flight. Fly only six roundtrips that were booked online and earn the same free trip (are they training us or what?). The free flights are simple to redeem (and transferable!) and are valid for *anywhere Southwest flies*. Hey, fly six trips between Reno and Vegas and head for Disney World, free!

The hallmarks of the Southwest Airlines Casino player reward program would be simplicity of use, ease of understanding and meaningful player rewards with meaningful choices of *value*. One point would equal one dollar of coin-in. Guests would have choices to spend their cash back or comp credit. There would be no more snarls because you were a table game player, or played different casino games or didn't visit for six months (hey, what happened to my point balance?). There'd be no more secrets — it would be a simple, but meaningful loyalty program that truly engendered loyalty.

Yes, I look forward to the first Southwest Airlines Casino. After all, we *are* in the flight business. We provide our guests flights of fancy and the freedom to escape on our amusement rides, hopefully with the everyday LUV we see so wonderfully and so consistently on Herb's marvelous Southwest Airlines.

"I love my job"

Her name is Julie. She is a masseuse at the spa in a downtown Reno casino where I like to play craps. She is a native born Nevadan and lives in a rural city, from where she drives three hours every Friday to spend the weekend kneading the sore and tired muscles of Reno gamblers. While Julie has been a masseuse most of her adult life, this is the first time she has ever worked at a casino.

And Julie gives the best massages I have ever had in my adult life.

Now don't get me wrong, I make no claim at being an expert on massage. Like most people, I get entirely too few massages. Even if we'd all like to have our bodies rubbed down every day, there is a certain limiting cost and time factor. But I'll bet I've had 100 or so massages in my life, so grant me that I know a good muscle minder when I see one, or rather, feel one.

And Julie is in a league by herself.

I discovered Julie almost by accident. A lucky run on the dice tables for a few weeks allowed me to accumulate quite a few comp dollars at this casino. As Reno is my hometown, I didn't need any hotel rooms and even my wife could stand only so many lobster dinners and bottles of wine with me at this casino's fine restaurant.

And then I discovered the spa. Thankfully, spa services were on the list of players club benefits (incredibly at some casinos with spas, they are not included as point perks), so I went up to the spa level of the hotel to claim my soothing largesse.

My first visit was non-eventful. The masseuse was fine — like dozens of others that I had encountered — and I certainly left the spa feeling refreshed. But frankly, it wasn't so refreshing that I would begin to spend any hard earned points there with reckless abandon.

On my second visit, I was assigned to Julie. She came into the quiet and dim waiting room and ascertained that I was her client (patient? customer?) and led me to the massage room. She wasn't gregarious, but carried a calm and assured manner that made me feel that my muscles and bones and joints were in for a rare treat.

I'll spare you from the "rub by rub" account of my first massage from Julie, but suffice it to say that the entire time, I had a smile on my face and knew I was in the hands (literally) of a true master of her craft.

And when my 60 glorious minutes of massage from Julie was completed, I had such a complete and relaxing glow over my entire body that I didn't want to leave. I could have dumped my entire comp point balance right on that massage table over the next few hours.

So I told Julie how great that experience was and what a marvelous skill she possessed. She stopped, looked me in the eye, thanked me for the compliment and said very directly and confidently "I *love* my job."

"I love my job." Those words stayed with me for the next several days as I pondered clients' dilemmas and pored over that pile of paper and legions of phone calls and pages of e-mails that we call "work."

"I love my job."

As I thought about the need for solid casino marketing strategic plans and effective use of marketing technology and the importance of creating customer loyalty, it occurred to me that perhaps it really might be as simple as finding casino employees who can "love their jobs" as much as Julie loves hers.

"I love my job."

It makes me wonder, if we asked all of our employees, "Do you love your job?" how many would honestly say yes? Would there even be one? I know we'd probably hear things about some uncaring supervisors, rules and procedures that inhibit serving guests, companies that utilize employees' bodies when they could get their minds and hearts too, for the same price.

"I love my job."

Is Julie just some random blessing that companies (if they are lucky) experience from time to time? In the real world, do we even think we can honestly weave enough managerial, or cultural or resourceful human magic that will make a cage cashier, a dealer, a security officer actually "love" their job?

I don't know.

But I do know that where the rare individual manager, or the rare department or the rare casino property, even the *very* rare casino company, truly cares about engaging its employees and making their work matter, then it really is possible to find employees who "love their jobs."

And for every Julie in our casino world, there will be hundreds of casino customers who will have experienced a marketing result that no ad, no players club, no loose slot machine and no direct mail offer could produce.

Thanks Julie, for loving your job and giving me something to take back to mine.

Marketing and disaster

When the good folks at *Casino Journal* told me they were doing a special issue on Hurricane Katrina and its effects on the Gulf Coast gaming industry, and that they would like me to contribute a column, I was excited … but sobered.

As *CJ*'s long-time marketing columnist, I realized something.

There were essentially no casinos left to market in the devastated area.

Certainly I could have chosen to write about reestablishing market position when the casinos reopen and the opportunities that would create. I could have written about the marketing opportunities in gaming towns like Tunica, Vicksburg or Philadelphia, Miss. Or appropriate advertising messages at such a difficult time.

But then I thought about the people. Not just the 10,000 homeless casino employees. But the good friends and associates who not only have helped my company prosper, but have become my friends.

There was Joe Billhimer, the GM at the Hard Rock in Biloxi, which was only a few days from opening when Katrina hit. How would he keep his team together? What would happen to the passion that Hard Rock was going to bring to the Gulf Coast?

There was Dane Turner of Ocean Springs, Miss., the president of SportGame, a gaming industry support company which conducts sports contests for casinos around the country, and whose house at one time during Katrina was a half-mile into the Gulf of Mexico. How would he continue to serve his dozens of clients (he did!) from his temporary refuge at a Holiday Inn Express in Dothan, Ala.? How would he get back to his home with the bridge destroyed and the roads in ruins and communication systems still down?

And then there was my good friend Deb Hilgeman, the editor of the *Mississippi Gaming News*. Knowing this wonderfully crazy lady, I could almost understand how she chose to stay in her beachfront Gulf Coast home and ride out Katrina. But I couldn't understand the sheer terror she must have felt watching her neighbors' homes swept past her, hearing her roof start to tear off, seeing her beloved dogs disappear and even after miraculously surviving, realizing she had lost everything.

I saw Deb Hilgeman at the Global Gaming Expo two weeks after Hurricane Katrina. She had two outfits to her name and was looking forward to buying a few more while in Las Vegas. She described to me her horrifying ordeal. She told me of the incredible hassles of dealing with FEMA. She wasn't sure what was going to become of her job or what she was going to do next.

But what struck me about Deb Hilgeman, all five feet of her, was the indomitable nature of the human spirit. She was glad to be alive and had a clear and renewed appreciation of life and what was really important. She was already thinking of her friends and neighbors who were not as fortunate as her. She was determined to move on with her life, whatever that meant.

Yes, I thought about Joe Billhimer and Dane Turner and Deb Hilgeman as I gathered my thoughts for this article that suddenly seemed so insignificant in comparison to what tens of thousands of gaming employees were experiencing right now. What could I possibly say that wouldn't sound trivial or meaningless to the craps dealers that entertained me at Grand Casino Biloxi? What could I do that might even make a small difference for the food servers that so graciously fed me at Casino Magic in Bay St. Louis? What would make any difference to the marvelous catering staff that had annually made the "Taste of the Gulf Coast" at the Southern Gaming Summit the finest party in the entire gaming industry?

For you see, while there may be stories and articles on the economic impact of Katrina on the gaming industry, on whether the Gulf Coast gaming market will come back in a land-based form or the time frames for reopening individual casinos, Katrina is still truly about people.

And right now, even as you read this, our gaming brothers and sisters continue to need our help. The national spotlight shines less bright and the sense of urgency to assist lessens. But even today, a dealer in New Orleans is trying to find a home while wages and benefits run out. A guest room attendant in Biloxi has buried three members of her family. A bartender in Gulfport looks for any job he can find while waiting, while hoping, for the casinos to reopen.

I applaud the efforts of the gaming companies who have responded so quickly and positively to the plights of their casino employees in the

Gulf Coast. And while their efforts are significant and important, it is not nearly enough. So I urge you to find some way to continue to help. Contribute to the American Gaming Association's Gaming Industry Katrina Relief Fund (www.americangaming.org). Respond to a request for help from the many casino companies seeking vendor support for their casino employees. If at all possible, find a job in your company for a displaced Gulf Coast gaming employee. And when that first casino reopens on the Mississippi Gulf Coast, prepare to take a trip and throw a few coins in those slot machines.

The people there will really appreciate it. It's called Southern Hospitality and it's our turn to show some to them.

My best marketing event ever

It started as my biggest flop and I was lucky I wasn't fired.

The time was the late-1980s and I was a junior marketing manager at the Harrah's property in Las Vegas. It was a heady time as I had recently been "discovered" by my mentor at the same time our casino embarked on an unprecedented surge in casino marketing activity. Prior to this point, our "marketing" consisted of loose dollar slots, a good, cheap buffet, friendly employees, a couple of slot hosts who conducted an annual slot tournament and a few yearly golf tournaments for (mostly) spoiled and unprofitable VIPs who worked the Strip casino golf circuit.

My mentor arrived from Atlantic City as the vice president of casino operations (with casino marketing under his charge), somewhat shocked by our lack of casino marketing activity. Why, in Atlantic City they had aggressive bus marketing, high-priced executive hosts, fancy VIP events, networks of junket reps, lavish cash offers sent in the mail, ethnic marketing programs and other marketing activities that made our novice efforts appear pretty meager (and I hadn't learned yet of the stupidity of Atlantic City "marketing wars").

So we cranked up our casino marketing machine — if you could call four people a machine. Where we did one slot tournament a year, we quickly got to doing one a month. We started having VIP parties regularly with name entertainers — OK, they were "B" entertainers, but to our unspoiled customers, they were pretty famous. We conducted major table game tournaments with prizes as high as $50,000, as well as thrice weekly "mini" 21 tourneys with buy-ins of $25 and first prize money of $1,000. We started bringing in junkets. We held an ESPN fight in a (too small) ballroom.

Through it all, I was encouraged to try new things that might have a casino marketing payoff. As I've had some crazy ideas in my time, this was like being a kid in a candy store, and the candy was *free*!

One of my earliest initiatives centered around a notion that I picked up as a table game floor person — namely that each floor manager personally knew dozens, if not hundreds, of casino customers. Maybe they were from the same hometown. Or the floor person reminded them of their son or daughter. Or the floor person (this is instant bonding) was the first one to turn the customer onto that magic word, "comp."

What if, I thought, we could get all of these casino floor executives to personally invite "their" customers to a VIP event? Wouldn't they all show up? And if we included their favorite Harrah's executive in the VIP event, wouldn't they have a great time and wouldn't that bond them even more to our casino hotel?

And that's how the Executive Invitational, the single best received and most profitable casino event I ever conducted, was born. And in its first year, it was a huge flop.

After conceiving the notion for the Executive Invitational, I went around to the various floor people and asked them if they would invite their "personal list" of good customers to a VIP event. "Isn't that your job?" some asked. "What's the event?" others wanted to know. Well since we had a golf event scheduled (and I was a golfer myself), I decided that the Executive Invitational was going to be a golf tournament. And any casino executive who could recruit at least four of their VIPs would get to play golf at the country club and host their players at the lavish parties. What an incentive! What a genius I was!

Only, most of our executives (and most of their customers) didn't play golf. And when only 12 guests showed up for the first Executive Invitational, I had produced an expensive flop that left me with serious egg on my polyester pants.

Although I should have given up on this "executives hosting customers" event, I didn't. "What activity would be of interest to both customers and executives?" I wondered. And then it hit me — why gambling, of course! The customers all gamble by definition. And of Las Vegas casino executives it's been said 99 percent of them gamble and the other 1 percent are liars!

So our Executive Invitational became a "team gambling event" where casino executives acted as captains and participants in a simple slot/blackjack team tournament with free credits and funny money chips. Each guest and each executive played one 15-minute slot tourney session and one 30-minute blackjack tourney session on the casino floor, which is exactly where we wanted them.

And the rest, as they say, is history. Five hundred VIPs showed up for the second Invitational, responding to an invitation signed by 12 senior property executives. Our best customers partied with 50 of our top executives, some of whom had never met, much less hosted, live, breathing VIP gamblers. They gambled together, they ate together, they drank together, they even sang together (yes, we had karaoke for our entertainment — customer and executive divisions, with an on-stage shower curtain for really shy crooners). Fifteen years later, Harrah's Las Vegas and the Rio continue to conduct the Executive Invitational, albeit in a somewhat different (but likely improved and more profitable) form.

All because a big flop didn't get me fired. And because pairing casino customers with casino executives carries the important marketing lesson that a piece of yourself is more valuable than a piece of your wallet.

My worst promotion ever

I've truly done some stupid things in my career. Well, they didn't seem so stupid when I did them, but it's funny how misguided assumptions, wildly optimistic goals and poor choices can conspire to bite you in the butt — every time.

The other day, I was pondering my all time stupid marketing endeavors and it made me wonder which one was at the top of my "hall of shame." And boy did I have some doozies to choose from:

There was the time we attempted to do slot jackpot celebrations by sprinkling "lucky dust" (gold and purple glitter meant to demarcate a winning slot area) right into a customer's eye.

I recall the "first ace" promotion, where we gave casino show go-ers a coupon good for a "first ace" as their initial card on a blackjack hand … only we didn't control the discarded coupons and scores of coupon hounds quickly found an effective way to get handfuls of coupons representing a 40 percent advantage.

There was the cooperative promotion with local McDonald's stores where we gave away free scratch off tickets good for free games in our casino's midway, meant for McDonald's customers (parents and kids), but somehow ending up in the pockets of gleeful McDonald's employees.

Then there was the time we sold bumper stickers and photos with strippers as a post 9/11 disaster relief fundraiser during the World Gaming Expo (that's a story for another time).

And of course I can't forget the time I made an appearance in a (too small) lobster costume at an employee fishing tournament.

Yes, I've certainly had more than my share of stupid promotions and endeavors. But nothing can match the time that I actually gave free rooms away to a good portion of the homeless population in downtown Reno.

It was called Winner Wonderland and it all started innocently enough. Our casino (like most casino hotels in North America) had a ton of empty rooms from Thanksgiving to Christmas. The idea was to fill those rooms by giving away two free room nights and a free entry into a specially-constructed, themed daily slot tournament that had $2,500 in daily cash prizes. I had successfully used this promotion at another property in Las Vegas, even winning a company award for its outstanding results.

The key in promoting a "Winner Wonderland" type promotion, where you are trying to attract customers at a time (the holidays) where they are not inclined to visit your casino, is to aggressively distribute invitations for the "two room night, two free slot tourney entry" offer. And for six months, we did. Every slot jackpot winner got an invitation to Winner Wonderland. Every new players club member who achieved even 50 points got an invitation to Winner Wonderland. We mailed Winner Wonderland invitations to our entire database. All our hosts and slot floor employees handed them out aggressively to active slot players at their own discretion.

Still, Winner Wonderland might have been successful, except for one fatal error. At our weekly strategic marketing meeting, when the GM asked how we were going to fill all the empty rooms not only in November and December, but also in January and February as well, I blurted out, "We'll just extend Winner Wonderland for two more months!" And so we did.

Now when Winner Wonderland is only a three- or four-week long promotion, it works just fine. Casino guests make an incremental visit during a really dead hotel occupancy period. Invitees, who normally don't receive free room offers or free shots at $2,500 in daily prize money, will respond in droves.

But when Winner Wonderland runs for three months instead of three weeks, a couple of things happen:

Players who would have come anyway during that three-month Winner Wonderland window now get a free room that they would have gladly and routinely paid for.

Scammers have enough time to figure out how to best take advantage of a very generous free room offer with a chance to win thousands in prize money daily.

At first, the results from Winner Wonderland that year looked promising. A few hundred rooms each night were filled with Winner Wonderland invitees and even though cash room sales were down, the gaming numbers looked pretty good. But as the weeks of Winner Wonderland wore on, the slot revenues were less and less inspiring.

One afternoon in late-January, I received a call from Reno's assistant chief of police, who informed me that our Winner Wonderland invitations (representing two free room nights) were "being used as currency" among Reno's homeless population who appreciated the lush digs and, for some of them, the free cash prizes to boot. At the weekly marketing meeting, the director of security admitted his staff was having numerous problems with some of the Winner Wonderland riff-raff, including one particular group of 10 stuffed into a one-bed room, who saw fit to cook on their hibachi grill right in the room (and boy did I hear about that for another year!).

To make a long story short, we cleaned up the Winner Wonderland operational mess and limped through the last three weeks of the promotion. We had made a little money, but not that much, and certainly not worth all of the work and aggravation. And although I should have sought some PR value for our housing many of Reno's homeless during the holidays, I let Winner Wonderland — my all time biggest loser — die a slow and quiet death.

But learn something I did, and that's why your biggest disasters can sometimes sow the seeds of some of your biggest triumphs. Just stay away from the name "Winner Wonderland." It still makes me cringe.

My biggest screw ups

Sure, I've had some successes in my 25 years in the gaming industry. They felt good. Sometimes people applauded. Once in a while there was a monetary payoff. But by far my greatest learning has come from screwing up.

That's right, poor decisions, unnecessary risks, tunnel vision, lazy thinking. You name it and I've probably used it to screw up. And not just little screw ups, but disastrous, life-threatening (well okay, maybe *career* threatening), royal *screw ups*.

And rather than entertain you with the screw ups of youth — even though the time that I told the neighborhood bully, Eddie Gaunder, that he was a bully, would be an entertaining story — I thought I would stick to my gaming screw ups.

So if confession is good for the soul, then here they are. My biggest screw ups and what I learned from them. Perhaps there are some lessons here for your Indian casino.

Screw up: *Quitting over principle*

Early in my gaming career, my wife and I were both working at a small little joint in a small Nevada town. We soon realized the money was in dealing. So we got to know the pit boss, practiced like hell and worked for free on live games (after shift and on our days off) to get dealing experience. When it came time to get hired, we were told that we'd have to wait because the owner had two women who had to get hired before us. The two women were mistresses of the owner. We quit that evening. Our dealing careers were derailed for a year and we had to move to another town.

Lesson: *Act on principle when you can make a difference.*

Screw up: *The confused client*

I had taken one of my first significant consulting jobs which entailed building a service evaluation mechanism for a large casino property about to open. The property had misjudged its customers and its community, was beset with operational issues and had inexperienced management. In essence, there was no service to evaluate as the organization had to go into crisis mode just to get open. My evaluation tool went unused. I received a big consulting check.

Lesson: *If you can't make a difference, don't stick around. You'll only add to the mess.*

Screw up: *Taking the money and running*

     Once I got serious about pursuing a career in gaming, my advancement happened fairly rapidly. I was with a top gaming company, I had several quick promotions and was told I had a bright future in senior management, probably as a general manager. A rival company offered to triple my salary if I would come help them "remake their culture." I accepted the offer. Within six months, new management came in, my position was eliminated and I was forced to fulfill my contract in another role with the company.

Lesson: *The grass may look greener, but first see what fertilizer they use.*

Screw up: *The winner is a loser*

     I had a great deal of success with a promotion called Winner Wonderland, where we gave free rooms and free slot tournament entries to players in order to fill rooms (and drive slot revenue) in December. Other casinos copied our successful promotion. When I moved to another gaming market, I reprised this promotion and ran it for three months instead of three weeks. We diluted the success and also got a black eye because local bums were showing up for their free rooms.

Lesson: *Don't mess with success, unless the formula you can bless (sorry).*

Screw up: *The false challenge*

     I was approached by two owner-operators to take over their distressed casino. I told them my radical plan for what would have to happen for it to survive. They were very interested in having me take the helm, but first they had to get a formal blessing from the casino's 88-year-old patriarch, which they assured me was not a problem. However, when he heard my "crazy" notions, he emphatically refused to let me run his baby. I wasted several weeks of work and preparation. The casino eventually closed.

Lesson: *Always be sure who is in charge before you cut a deal.*

Screw up: *The kiddie promotion*

I was working for a casino that had a very popular midway area for kids and families. I theorized that if we could use the midway to attract kids then they would drag their parents in who would spend time in the casino while the kids played the games. We partnered with three local McDonalds restaurants, which handed out scratch cards (good for at least one free game at our midway) with every purchase. We were inundated with people in our midway — mostly McDonald's employees and their friends who had grabbed scratch cards by the handful. We cancelled the promotion in two weeks.

Lesson: *Don't forget who your real customers are.*

Embrace your screw ups. If you make no mistakes, you're not learning.

Million-dollar marketing ideas

It is somewhat against my better judgment to be handing out million-dollar marketing ideas for free. After all, a consultant's gotta make a living.

But some of this stuff is so simple and so powerful that I just can't hold my tongue any longer. Maybe you've already discovered these million-dollar marketing bonanzas at your casino or maybe you've just scratched the first few thousand bucks of their million-dollar potential. Or maybe, heaven forbid, you disagree with my million-buck assessment or you feel other factors override the revenue potential. That's OK, I've been wrong before.

However, let's be clear on the million-dollar terms — if you follow my advice on Monday, you won't have the million on Friday. And of course, this all depends on the size of your gaming operation — if you have a hundred gaming positions at your gaming facility, getting the million will take longer, of course.

But all else being equal, assuming you have a moderate-sized gaming operation, that the suggestions all apply and that you are not already taking advantage of them, then *all of these notions should be worth a million bucks (or more) to your casino in the next one to two years.*

So here they are, my "Million-Dollar Marketing Ideas:"

1. ***Get more penny slot machines and dump some one dollar slots*** — I've been to enough casinos to confidently make this statement. Players are waiting in line to play penny games and the dollar games are often empty. And the WPU (win per unit) from the pennies rivals results from strong 25-cent and $1 games. So grab your million if you have any cents.

2. ***Get shuffling machines for your "21" games; for craps shooters who "set the dice," when they shoot them, have your craps stickpersons deliver the dice "pre-set" to these shooters; eliminate the "No Mid-Entry" rule at "21" games; and stop every table game procedure (checking currency with counterfeit-sensing pens, calling out "change $50," "clocking the drop," stopping a game for "the count," etc.) that slows a game down***

or prevents (or delays) table game players from playing — I have lumped all of these table game million-dollar marketing ideas together, and boy can I hear the uproar from the security-conscious table game VPs already! I don't care. All the aforementioned "rules and procedures" do is slow the games down and cost you money! Hey, find other (and cheaper) ways to catch the bad guys — we're talking millions here!

3. *Charge for your hotel rooms by the hour, instead of by the day* — Now bear with me on this one. I'll leave it to *you* to figure out *how* to do this, but when you accomplish the hourly standard, here's what should happen:

•   You'll figure out how to have your guest rooms cleaned more efficiently on a rolling time frame and not by that dreaded "not ready to be occupied before 3:00 p.m." standard.

•   You'll create an incentive for guests to check out early, allowing a "quicker turn" of the rooms (isn't that the principle used to increase restaurant profits???).

•   You'll have a strong marketing advantage with guests who want to arrive late or leave early!

    If this isn't a million-dollar idea, I don't know what is! So can you book me for 11:00 p.m. to 8:00 a.m. for New Year's? And I don't care if you gouge me for the nine hours!

4. *Get some great CRM software and use it!* — I won't give you any recommendations here, even though I have my personal favorites. But the concept is, if you don't have a full picture of your casino customers and all of the cash registers where they spend money with you, then you're missing out on millions. Ask Harrah's!

5. *Let all of your best slot customers play every new slot machine before it hits your casino floor for free in demo mode* — I don't

care if you do this through private VIP "New Slot" parties, or a special demo area on the casino floor or even as free play credits on live casino slots (you might check out the Acres system for this), just do it! You do want your best customers sampling your new games, don't you? And I could give you a million reasons why that is a good idea.

6. ***Put retail items for sale where your customers would least expect them (and might buy them)!*** — This isn't just the logo beer mugs for sale at the sports bar, it's a *retail crusade*. It's commemorative chips and tokens for sale at the cage; cards/dice/chips/dealer shirts for sale in the pit; an assortment of unique salsas for sale in your new southwestern restaurant; it's espresso, hard candies and hot towels for sale near the slots; concert tickets for sale at the front desk. And I could give you a million other examples!

7. ***Have each of your top 10 gaming executives personally spend an hour per year with a 100 of your top 1,000 customers*** — Whether that time is spent over dinner, or at a VIP event or visiting them at their business — *wherever* — this is not just worth a million, it's darn near priceless! For cementing relationships with the 20 percent of your customers who drive 80 percent of your business, heck, that's the stuff millionaires are made of!

So there you have them, seven of my best "Million-Dollar Marketing Ideas" at no charge. But the Billion-Dollar Ideas, I'm keeping for myself.

The slot celebration that backfired

Nowadays, you're apt to see a lot of things that casinos do to celebrate their slot jackpot *winners'* good fortune (although as an industry, I don't think we do near enough for our slot *losers*). Many casinos take photos of their jackpot winners. "Wall of Winners" displays are now very common. Jackpot winner parties are routinely used to invite back the lucky slot players and celebrate en masse their good fortune. Many slot marketers will hand winners some branded trinket which players can wear, hang, display or otherwise advertise on behalf of the casino where they "got lucky."

But such wasn't always the case. There once was a time when slot jackpot winners got little more than a blaring eruption from a slot machine's jackpot bell "assault weapon" and a cash payoff some 30 minutes later.

Consider this a piece of gaming history. It is the story of one of the first "slot celebrations" in the gaming industry, a study in the process of innovation and a lesson in Murphy's Law or "what can go wrong, probably will."

The time was 1992 and the place was Harrah's Las Vegas. I was the casino marketing manager and after much deliberation, our property had just undergone a name change, going from the Holiday Casino to Harrah's Las Vegas. (Lots of discussion about our "brand"). Our slot director was Tom Jenkin, now a senior muckety-muck with Harrah's, but back then a gaming greenhorn who nonetheless intuitively knew that our business was all about slots. As my new boss, Tom made it clear to me that we were going to focus on our slot players and he wanted my department's efforts to reflect that.

Every so often, I would be given some vague executive direction on slot marketing strategy and be asked to "come up with something." Once I was asked to make our successful slot tournaments more efficient … another time, to come up with a concept of a sports-themed slot area. And then, "make the experience for our slot jackpot winners a memorable one."

Now I was a pretty creative guy, but I have always found that if you can gather a good group of people that will spark off each other then the creative process will be far superior to attempting innovation by

132

yourself. So we established a Slot Marketing Creative Committee, looking for intelligent, well-spoken, slightly off-kilter, employees (from any department) who were *slot players themselves* (you should do this). And one of the first issues our group noodled on was how to create a great slot celebration for our jackpot winners.

After kicking around dozens of ideas from the practical to the wacky, we decided that the ultimate slot celebration had to have the following elements: an over-the-top festive ceremony, music, a crowning gift, a mystical aura of "luck" and a photograph to commemorate the whole thing.

Here's how we had planned it to work. The slot employee who first happened upon the jackpot would be required to go get the paperwork and the cash payoff. So we established "celebration stations" near where this employee had to travel anyway, asked him or her to grab a boom box, a small Polaroid camera, a winner's medallion and a small packet of "Lucky Dust" at the station. The employee was to turn on the boom box loudly (we used the song "Celebrate" by Kool and the Gang) and have the music follow him to the jackpot site. Before paying out the cash, the slot employee was to crown the winner by placing a gold medallion around the winner's neck (we stole the medallion idea from Caesars Palace, which used it as an incentive for initial play from new players club members). Then they were to hand the winner the packet of purple and teal (Harrah's colors at the time) "Lucky Dust" (which was just colored glitter) in case the winner wanted to sprinkle the Lucky Dust in the area to demarcate the winning spot for others walking by. The cash payoff was then to be counted out in the winner's hand enthusiastically with a photo then taken to commemorate the whole winning event.

At least that's the way it was supposed to happen.

On the day of our scheduled trial run of our jackpot celebration concept, the creative committee was eager with anticipation. All of the elements were put in place and we had worked with the slot employees to explain the concept and get their buy-in. We hit a little snag with the Lucky Dust, which was supposed to be a small neatly packaged plastic bag of glitter with a mystical winning message attached to it. The vendor had not yet delivered the little Lucky Dust packets, so we used some little ketchup cups from the employee's cafeteria, put in the glitter ourselves and told the slot employee on their first trial run to hand this "Lucky

Dust" to the jackpot winner and have her throw it into the air in joyous, glittery celebration.

After several minutes of waiting, we got our first jackpot announced on the slot department walkie-talkie. We watched in great glee and anticipation. The boom box and the playing of "Celebrate" loudly was a stroke of genius — slot players all craned their necks to see what was going on. Our first jackpot winner loved the commemorative gold medallion and winner's photo. The money was counted out enthusiastically and with great flair. What a celebration we had created — we would be property heroes!

And then the jackpot winner was handed the ketchup-cup full of purple and teal glitter, was told to throw it into the air to "mark" this lucky spot and flicked it over her shoulder right into the eyes of the player on the adjoining slot stool.

The lady was OK, the paramedics came and rinsed out her eyes and we didn't get sued.

And our slot celebration took root as a signature event at Harrah's Las Vegas, after this very inauspicious start.

But we never let our slot winners throw glitter in the air again.

Tony, the midget shoeshine man

I swear the following story is true. But it will sound so unbelievable that you may question my sanity. However I guarantee that there will be several lessons here for your casino — even if you don't have a shoeshine stand at your property.

Tony is a midget. Even though there may be a more politically correct term, he assures me that "midget" is what he prefers to be called. Tony works at a shoeshine stand at a major Las Vegas Strip casino-hotel. The stand is in a poor location and you could actually miss it if you weren't looking for it.

My business associate and I were doing some work in Las Vegas and happened to be staying at the casino hotel where Tony had his shoeshine stand. We had just finished a long day and were heading back to our rooms. I just happened to take a glance and noticed the shoe shine stand as we were passing. Our shoes were dusty from the long Las Vegas day and seeing a midget shining shoes naturally piqued our curiosity. I remember thinking how ergonomically correct it all seemed since Tony did not have to bend down to do his cleaning and shining.

We agreed to stop even though there was a shoeshine customer currently being serviced and we would have to wait. Tony barked out a welcome as he introduced himself. He talked with a heavy Italian accent and I guessed that he was probably 60 years old with tough, leathery skin that fit his chosen profession well. Tony told us that he would be a little while longer and then went back to his non-stop conversation with his current shoeshine customer.

It took Tony at least 20 more minutes before he turned to my associate and me. In that time I discovered he had been married eight times, had 11 children and several grandchildren, spoke nine languages, leased this shoeshine stand and owned a leather repair store in town. I watched as he offered to shine a second pair of shoes and treat the leather jacket of his current customer. Our wait sped by as we were absolutely enthralled by this midget shoeshine man and his obvious passion for leather and customers.

My turn was next and I watched in awe as Tony began by setting his liquid polish applicator on fire and then lighting the entire rim of my shoe soles (to open up the leather's pores). My associate and I had an amazed laugh with each other, and then my associate said, "The only thing that could be better than this would be to have a beer right now."

"Wait right here while I get you a beer," ordered Tony. "What kind would you like?"

At that point, he took his own money, walked over to an idle tour desk representative and asked her to run and get two beers for us at the nearest bar. He came back immediately to keep shining my shoes. And instruct me on the various virtues and proper care of leather.

Tony didn't use a rag to rub the black cream polish into my shoes. He used his hands. With a rag, he explained, most of the polish went into the rag and not into the shoes.

My shoe shine took nearly 30 minutes and in that time I heard Tony's philosophy on women, children, life, Las Vegas, Hollywood, the value of foreign languages and, especially, the proper care of leather. He offered to treat my leather briefcase and my other pair of shoes that were in my room. He bought us a second round of beers. He spoke honestly about the challenges (and benefits) of being a midget. He charged me twice as much as a normal shoeshine and I would have paid twice as much again.

Of course I stayed for my associate's shoeshine to hear more from this giant of a person, who also happened to be the best entertainment in Las Vegas at that moment.

So OK Dennis, you're thinking, what does the story of Tony the midget shoeshine man have to do with my casino?

First of all, it's all about entertaining customers and being that gaming is an experience, that should be a goal and a focus for your casino. Imagine how loyal your table games customers would be if each one was a Tony with their customers!

Second, all of your employees should be salespeople for your organization. Tony didn't just shine my shoes, he offered me other products and services and really sold me on the casino. Plus he increased beer revenue!

Third, Tony illustrates well that even a menial task in a lousy location can translate into a huge success if you add a little passion. So what have you done lately to kindle the passion in your gaming employees???

And finally, the lesson of this story is that if a midget lights your shoes on fire, don't worry, as long as the shoes are leather and the midget is as wonderfully knowledgeable as Tony.

Strategy ~ Philosophy

Some thoughts on branding

I have found it to be valuable in my career to admit when something confuses me. For a long time, the mindset of the slot player was a mystery to me, but after years of talking to those folks and yes, even sampling the continuing avalanche of new slot games, I think I "get" slots.

Advertising continues to puzzle me. I mean, I find some advertising to be entertaining, some to be informative and, I hate to admit this, but a certain amount of advertising is probably *necessary*. I just don't know how much is necessary and how you measure what advertising you do have.

For me, the same holds true for branding. While I wouldn't consider myself an advertising or a branding expert, I do believe that over the past three decades in the casino business, I have gained a good, basic grasp of what branding is. Your "brand" is simply how you are perceived in the marketplace by customers and potential customers. It speaks to every aspect of your business — advertising, facility, games, employees, look, feel, you name it — and it speaks to a *feeling* — how you are perceived in the customer's mind. And if I have learned anything in this crazy casino marketing biz, it is that what brand a casino organization thinks it has and what brand its customers perceive it having are often very different.

These are the "brand variations" that I currently see in vogue in casinos (and if you firmly believe that your casino's brand is terrifically unique, I am sorry to reduce it to a category):

The gamblin' joint — If you are a player, a real player, this is your casino. It gives you a fair shake for your money. Low minimums, high limits, liberal gaming odds. The promotions offer real value. If you play, you are taken care of. Some examples of this brand would be the Horseshoe Casinos, Barona Valley Ranch Resort & Casino, Club Cal Neva in Reno and a few others on both the high and low end. Frankly, I'm surprised we don't see more examples of this brand. It sure seems to speak to the reason why many people partake in this crazy activity called *gambling*.

The entertainment center — In this very common casino branding, you almost wouldn't know there was a casino involved. It is the full range of the "entertainment experience" that is being branded — the restaurants, the shows, the retail shops, the spa, the hotel, the golf course and every other amenity there. In Las Vegas, this is the next brand evolution. In other gaming markets, it is the first brand evolution from the "gambling center" concept. This certainly is the brand with the broadest appeal and in many of these "entertainment centers" (especially in Las Vegas), gambling revenue may even be less than 50 percent of the total resort revenue.

The fun place — This attempted casino brand stresses that this casino is "more fun" than others. It implies that more people win there and enjoy it more when they do. It implies that the employees there are more fun as well and like to party with guests. This brand "implies" a lot about the experience you can expect there and, from my experience, usually doesn't deliver.

Where locals play — This is the casino brand that usually attempts to distinguish itself in a crowded field by being the choice of savvy, regular, nearby players. It often highlights the "value" in what matters to these insiders — food value, gaming value (loose slots, frequent winners, etc.), promotion value, etc. This brand has elements of the "fun place" casino brand, but typically highlights more of its (cheaper) price elements and the imputed endorsements of regular local players.

The upscale experience — This brand is Bellagio, Wynn and Caesars Palace (among a few others) in Las Vegas, but it's also some elite European-style casinos, even a Seminole Hard Rock in Florida. This brand is classy, almost elegant. It's where the "beautiful people" play. While it may not have many more experiences than the typical casino or resort casinos, it executes them with more style. This brand targets a wealthy demographic that is not interested in price if they feel they can get uncommon value.

Unfortunately, most casinos have no brand, a weak brand or a constantly shifting hodgepodge of brand elements from those common brands identified here. Consequently they try to be too many things to too many people, and ultimately don't strike a brand chord with anyone.

As I mentioned, I am not a casino "brand expert." I am not sure what brand is best. I don't know the secret, most effective brand awareness building formula (if there is one) for your casino. But I do think I know this about casino brands: if your customers are routinely saying things like "I feel I can win there" and "I feel comfortable there" and "They listen to me" and "The people there are so nice," then you have a pretty damn strong brand.

Or maybe it's not a brand at all, just a nifty way of doing business whereby what matters to your customers and employees is much more important than a P&L, or a casino operating rule or some hi-falutin' (and expensive) branding image and campaign.

The concept of stalled revenue streams

Casino marketing is typically about growing casino revenue. Sometimes, truth be told, in highly-competitive markets, casino marketing may be about slowing the decline in casino revenue. And nowadays, in the modern-day casino resort, casino marketing can even be about growing revenues in areas outside of the casino like hotel, food and beverage, retail or entertainment. Hey, we don't care what cash register the money goes into!

But normally, casino marketing is about selling more casino gambling to casino customers. And usually that marketing falls under the categories of acquisition, retention, growth and reactivation.

Casinos do a lot of marketing around acquisition, even if sometimes there are few customers in a locale left to acquire. Heavy advertising, buying lists, bus marketing, junket rep development and big club-wide promotions often have acquisition as a goal.

Retention and growth are also common casino marketing strategies and many casinos have become more sophisticated at it in recent years. Usually direct mail campaigns, VIP events, play-extending casino floor promotions and even the players club itself, have retention and growth as goals. Keep what you have and incent them to play a little more.

There is less activity around reactivation and I'm not sure why that is. Oh sure, most casino marketing efforts include a "Come Back, Where the Heck Ya Been?" mailing to inactives or sometimes even some telemarketing, but from my experience, reactivation is either neglected or not pursued aggressively enough. Hey, they were customers once!

So acquisition, retention, growth and reactivation are the standard objectives of most casino marketing efforts today, but I have been noodling lately on a concept that I feel has long been ignored, has immediate payback and just might make you a casino marketing star. It's the concept of "stalled revenue streams" and heck, let's call it SRS and maybe it can take its place among CRM, RFM, ROI and other casino marketing acronyms.

The concept of stalled revenue streams is simple: find an area in your gaming operation where customer spending is reduced, slowed or stopped altogether and *fix it!* And while that may not be as exciting as doing a direct mail campaign with 100 segmentation levels, I assure you that it may have an equally-large impact on gaming revenue.

So you don't know where your SRSs are? Well not to worry, I've been noticing this stuff, as well as the progressive casinos that are doing something about them. And here are some of the key dammed-up streams:

Players leaving their slot machines to go eat — This may be the biggest SRS of all. Players get hungry and leave their slot machine. Yes, some players want to take a break and dine, but others would gladly munch while they play. And casinos like Barona Valley Ranch, Three Rivers in Oregon, Gold Dust West in Reno and several others are now offering slot-side dining. And so should you — revenue stream un-stalled!

Lines at ATMs — Most casinos have two or three ATMs (bigger casinos may have six or eight) and when it's busy, it becomes a big SRS. Players in lines are not *spending*. And that applies to restaurant lines (give 'em a beeper!), cage lines, show lines, any lines at all. But Barona has dozens of ATMs (no waiting!) and other casinos have also attacked various lines with pagers, more innovative use of staff, process re-design, line passes and a host of "SRS attack devices."

Holding slot machines for players taking a break — This is a tricky SRS as (good) players do take breaks from extended slot play and don't want others hijacking the machine that they have "primed." Now I'm not saying you shouldn't reserve a player's slot machine, but you may think creatively here to unplug this SRS. What about paying the player to allow someone else to play the slot during his or her break? What about variable incentives to get the breaking player back sooner? What about signs to quickly direct players to a *non-reserved* slot machine of the same denomination and model?

SRS technology snags or inefficiencies — Bill validators with less than optimal acceptance rates; kiosks that don't work half the time; ticket printers that are jamming more than the industry standard — fix these snags and more and you'll have customers playing more and grappling with technology less.

Uncomfortable playing experience — This could be painful slot stools, or drafty playing areas or surly dealers that run off players. In fact, you may not even notice these stalled revenue streams because they have the trappings of "normal business."

Stalled revenue streams are insidious. And while it may not be as sexy to address SRSs as conduct a $1 million casino promotion, unclogging these revenue streams may just be the most valuable marketing result you can achieve at your casino. So start flushing!

Growth strategies for flat markets

It is no secret that the growth of gaming has slowed in the past year. Sure, there are still some great opportunities in North America, specifically on the tribal gaming and racino fronts, and worldwide there are several potentially lucrative gaming markets still untapped. But in the United States anyway, whether it's because of rapid expansion, a slowing economy, the war or just the "bloom being off the (gambling) rose," many casinos in many different markets are now grappling with how to grow their gaming business.

Working in many of these slow growth gaming markets for the past five years has given me (I think) a unique perspective on these "marketing for growth" strategies that I have seen. Although each casino in each gaming market tends to have somewhat unique characteristics and circumstances, their responses to flat growth can be lumped under a few broad marketing strategies:

Build it and they will come — This is the expansion strategy, adding more casino floor space, building golf courses and hotels and entertainment venues, adding additional casinos in existing communities or on existing reservations. It's a risky, expensive tactic that can have a big payoff if a gaming company has done its homework. But as often as not, this strategy has led to disappointing returns on investment.

Let's advertise — This strategy usually involves a significant increase in advertising expenditures or in the amount of advertising in heretofore untapped (and usually far-flung) markets. Rarely have I seen this approach work, mostly because many casinos' advertising budgets are already severely bloated and few casinos tie in their advertising to driving measurable gaming activity.

Give away the store — You see this approach very often in very competitive markets (Atlantic City, Las Vegas locals' casinos, the Gulf Coast, etc.). One casino starts double point days, another does triple point days. One gives away a car, another a car a week, a third a car a day. A clear attempt to buy market share, I have never seen this tactic work. Typically each competitor in this type of marketing war ends up paying more money for the same customers.

Buying new business — This marketing strategy assumes there are big pockets of untapped business still out there (even though the casino has been around for 10 years now). Here you will see list buying, prospect mailings, bringing in bus business and signing on with junket reps. While I have seen this approach find a sliver of new business here or there, it is typically expensive and ill advised.

Zero in on the database — This strategy is usually an attempt to grow business by using more focused tactics on known customers of known worth. Usually this involves increased marketing budgets for direct mail, use of e-mail, casino promotions (for active players), the "one company, one card" approach and a variety of other focused strategies. I actually like this strategy when it is coupled with a corresponding decrease in other less-focused, less-measurable casino marketing tactics — and when it is not done to excess.

Do nothing — Yes, this is a casino marketing strategy for flat markets and as its name implies, you literally "do nothing" (or at least nothing additional) from a marketing perspective. Surprisingly, this can be a good strategy when all of the competitors are collectively jerking their knees and giving away the store, but can hurt business when smart competitors have found ways to nibble away at your market share.

Improve customer service — Except for Harrah's (as a company) and a few savvy individual casinos, you rarely see service used as a weapon in flat gaming markets. And that's too bad, for this "soft" tactic that is so underappreciated and misunderstood, can have a "hard" payoff in customer retention, which is a desirable result, especially in a tough market.

Collectively, I realize this summary of casino marketing strategies for flat markets doesn't paint a real flattering picture. But hey, that's why they are flat gaming markets! If it was simple, you'd continue to see explosive growth in Atlantic City or Biloxi. On top of that, as a young industry, most casinos started in a monopoly-like, or at least an under-served, gaming market. The pickins have been easy — 'til now.

But there is one casino market growth strategy that you never see and that's a property-wide, coordinated, strategic, *sales* effort. What is that? It's McDonald's asking, "Do you want fries with that?" It's Red Lobster asking if you want (for only 99 cents) shrimp on your dinner salad. It's The Men's Warehouse suggesting "a few nice ties" to go with that suit you just purchased. *It's getting your casino employees to suggest and recommend ways for your casino customers to more fully enjoy your products and services (and of course spend more money with you).*

And the first casino in each flat gaming market that figures out how to do this, how to *sell* to its casino customers, comprehensively, effectively and beneficially (for the casino, its customers and its employees), will have a strong leg up on growing business in these tough times.

But how do you build this sales culture into your casino operation? I'm not sure, I haven't done it and except for a few isolated casino examples (food servers pushing wine sales, room reservationists suggesting upgrades, etc.), I haven't seen it either. But I'm guessing it will take leadership, training, a significant budget, a revised focus, unrelenting inspection and significant employee incentives.

But what this sales strategy will look like is pretty clear to me. It will be your security officer at the front door recommending I try your delicious buffet. It will be your blackjack dealer *asking me* if I want to sit down and try my luck. It will be your slot change person promoting the progressive jackpot on carousel five. It will be your hotel clerk insisting I just have to see your great new show.

And it will be *you* realizing that tough times call for a renewed understanding and appreciation of all the great things we have to sell in our casinos. Think about it.

Leveraging your marketing experts

Everyone is an expert on marketing, especially in the casino industry. Casino employees who would never say two words about blackjack game spreads, slot machine mix or cashier cage location know *exactly* where your casino should have billboards and what kinds of promotions you should run on midweek mornings. If you don't believe me, ask them.

This "know-it-all" attitude on casino marketing is not necessarily a bad thing for your employees or non-marketing executives to have. In fact, you can build on this innate interest in marketing to create a much more customer-focused marketing organization for your casino. And here are the important points to share with your budding marketing gurus so that they can be more than armchair marketing experts:

The definition of marketing — When they see in Webster's Dictionary that "marketing" is defined as: *All business activity involved in the moving of goods (or services) from the producer to the consumer, including selling, advertising, packaging, etc.*, a light bulb usually goes off in every employee that alerts them that, "Hey, I'm in marketing, too!" Be sure to highlight the words "All" and "etc." in the definition.

The "80-20" rule — You know, the Pareto Principle, whereby approximately 20 percent of our casino's customers account for 80 percent of its profitability. This is a good time to make the point that, "we are in the business of being nice to people for money, the more money they have, the nicer we are!"

The concept of lifetime worth — Most casino employees are startled when they see that a "5-cent Sadie" can have tens or hundreds of thousands of dollars of worth to a casino over her lifetime. It helps send the message that every customer is important and if you lose one, you're losing more than a $20 bill.

The "best" marketing tactics — This one is a little more difficult because many casino executives themselves don't know what the best marketing tactics are. But casino employees tend to equate good marketing with good advertising; consequently they tend to look at mass-media visibility (radio, TV, newspaper, billboards, etc.) as the measure of a casino's marketing prowess. Inform them as to the higher value of direct mail, a players club, casino promotions for casino players and (especially) customer service.

The value of great customer service — Most employees intuitively know the value of great customer service — increased loyalty, word of mouth, guest satisfaction, etc. — but they are not often made fully aware of the value of great customer service for *them*. Better wages, better tips, greater job security, better working environments, etc., etc., etc. So tell them!

The customer experience — Oftentimes casino employees believe their job is to make the general manager, their department head, their shift manager or their immediate supervisor happy. They really need to see that their job is (as Isle of Capri Casinos so aptly says) to "Just Please the Guest!"

Why promotions are being done and why the employee role in them is so important — "Internal" marketing around casino promotions typically involves giving employees an oversized button to wear on their uniforms (they *hate* those!) and an information sheet on the promotion which is usually posted on some little-read employee bulletin board. Why not gather their input in the design of the promotion and create an *employee* component to the casino promotion that mirrors the *customer* component? I often see casinos spend a million dollars on a big, splashy promotion and then a few hundred bucks on communicating the promotion to the employees who are supposed to sell it.

Your casino's marketing strategy — Those new bus groups that show up at the casino on Tuesdays, or those blackjack coupons that start appearing in droves in the table game areas, or that sports cap giveaway that has customers lined up at the players club — these and other marketing initiatives can appear to casino employees as nothing more than ill-conceived operational snafus if you don't explain where they fit into your casino's marketing strategy. "Oh, I see we're running a test on Tuesdays with charter buses to see if we can attract new customers at an opportune time!"

If you can educate your employee "marketing experts" and take advantage of their inherent interest in marketing, you will be that much closer to being a customer-focused marketing organization. And remember, employees are customers too, and they deserve to understand what this "marketing stuff" is all about. It can only help your marketing efforts and might even develop some true marketing experts among the troops.

Working weekends as a marketing tool

It was a late Sunday morning and I was flying out of a resort destination airport. With many tourists flying home after the busy weekend, naturally the airport was crowded and business was very brisk in the various airport shops and concessions. I walked into the nearest news/gift shop to buy a bottle of water for the flight and I was immediately struck by the very long line snaking out into the concourse. Only one (of three) cash registers was open and the busy Sunday volume of purchases clearly overwhelmed the single, harried cashier. Clearly this airport shop was understaffed and/or the flow of business was being mismanaged.

Well of course this got me thinking about casinos, which also have definite peaks and valleys in their business flows. In fact, it is fair to say that most casinos get 60 percent (or more) of their weekly business in a 48-hour period from Friday evening to Sunday evening. If you exclude weekend graveyard times (if the casino is open 24 hours), then the business rush is even more compacted.

That makes it even more astounding to me that so many senior casino executives have weekends off.

I know I am about to get in hot water and generate hate mail from some well-meaning, hard-working, nine-to-five, Monday-to-Friday casino executives. I don't care. My role here is to point out things that can help your marketing efforts and make your casino guests happier.

I have become familiar now with the organization and inner workings of well over 100 casinos. Certainly some have "all hands on deck" on weekends but it is more common to see no more than one or two members of a 10-member senior management team *ever* work regularly on Saturdays or Sundays (and most vacate the property early on Fridays before the casino gets real busy). Usually those "weekend warriors" are the slots and table games execs. You almost never see a CFO, or an HR vice president or a chief engineer in the joint on weekends. Sometimes you'll see a GM (either feeling guilty or showing a token amount of support for the weekend weary troops) make an effort to show up on property for a few hours every Saturday (early) evening. That usually makes a few other managers magically show up during that time as well.

I have asked myself many times why so many gaming managers get so scarce when so many customers are clearly so present. The answers,

I'm afraid, are very unsettling. Some managers don't view their role as having to be on the casino floor interacting with customers. Others are shy or feel they have already put in their time in the trenches. Too many don't like the kinds of people that make up the majority of our customers, or they think gambling is stupid.

I have seen several casino organizations try to address this "casino manager disappearing act" by mandating that managers work on Saturdays, or they create a revolving "manager on duty" position and ask senior managers to take turns filling it. I guess this is better than nothing. But as often as not, I see managers filling this duty by hanging out in their office or in the back of the casino coffee shop. One time, Jim Hughes, then the GM at Palace Station in Las Vegas, changed the locks on all of the doors of his senior managers' offices to send the message that he needed them to be on the floor with customers — after a roof collapse and partial flooding occurred in the casino. That would be a neat approach to the weekend issue.

And what is really interesting is that I have yet to meet a casino executive who *doesn't* acknowledge the wisdom of working weekends and readily admit they would like to spend more time with customers. So what gives here? Is this just a case of the spirit being willing and the flesh being weak?

Well, if you agree with me so far (and aren't calling me a home wrecker for suggesting you cut into your kids' soccer time or dance lessons to spend time in a smoky casino on Saturdays), then let me suggest the following:

Don't mandate working weekends. Just start showing up yourself and model the behavior you desire, especially that which involves interacting with customers.

Look for creative ways to combine work and family on weekends. Take your spouse to the casino gourmet room and slip away on the casino floor while he or she plays the slots. Invite your kids to the concert and sit with some VIP customers. Stay in the hotel with the family as an in-town weekend getaway. You get the picture.

Break your routine and force yourself to interact with customers. If all you do on Saturdays is trudge into your office to pore over more reports and graphs and budgets, then you might as well stay home on weekends. The casino floor is where it's at!

Touch your employees. And whether that involves pitching in when it gets busy (and boy is it busy on weekends!), or working a formal shift for a front liner as a form of reward or just spending some time with the troops in the EDR — just do it!

Use the experience to improve your organization. On weekends, many of your business systems are operating at capacity and your employees are working at another level and another speed. Use your "weekend working" to pinpoint operational problems and suggest solutions. You'll never get that chance on dayshift weekdays because as one of my mentors once said, "Hey, we're real good when no one's here!"

Working weekends is an acquired habit. Once you start doing it, you won't mind it. And the mark you make with your customers and employees will make you realize that joining the weekend fray at your casino is one of the most powerful marketing efforts you can undertake.

Marketing styles

I have worked with lots of different casino marketing executives in my career. Heck, I have been one of them myself. And one thing these folks will never be accused of is being clones of each other. Talk about characters! I'll bet if you looked into the right sides of their brains, you'd see something from one of those kids' kaleidoscopes.

Marketing is an interesting department in which to work. There are opportunities to be creative and often the marketing budgets are more than ample (there is a point to be made here, but I won't go there). And marketing often is a lot of fun, where casino marketing execs regularly get to party with casino customers (the security guy or HR gal can't say that). The marketing department is also one area where qualified women might (remember, I said "might") be able to break the organizational glass ceiling a little more easily.

On the downside, working in marketing can involve incredibly long and irregular hours. There can be a lot of heat when business gets soft or a casino competitor down the street starts "giving away the store." Marketing tends to get all of the blame and little of the credit for a casino's success. And it is common knowledge that "marketing" is the one area where nearly every employee has an opinion — what ads the casino should be running, what promotions will pack the joint, how to get players to come in on graveyard, etc.

Yes, marketing is not an easy gig, and as I was pondering on the thousands of hard working professionals who toil in this arena, it occurred to me that while they may be as unique as snowflakes, different marketing executives can fairly be classified by their different styles. Here are the various marketing styles that I believe are prevalent in the modern day casino:

The 'bean counter' — This is a rare marketing style, even though every casino executive believes marketing should drive revenue and be measurable. For whatever reason, left brain accountants tend to not gravitate into marketing. More often marketing will be given an "analyst" to help it sort through the numbers. But occasionally a bean counter lands in marketing and this style is categorized by poring over reports, cranking out analysis and generally trying to add science to the marketing function. The bean counter spends 70 percent of her time at a computer terminal and the other 30 percent in meetings. Rarely will you see her on the casino floor.

The 'media personality' — This is the ex-TV news personality or radio DJ who jumped over to gaming when the new casino hit town. The glitz and glamour of the casino lights attracted him and he assumed it would be a great, fun job. He has numerous contacts in the media and the community so all casino events are "splashy" and high profile. He doesn't really understand the gaming business but figures the old casino veterans will handle their end of the business while he handles his.

The 'trainee' — This marketing style is fairly common at tribal casinos. It usually involves an intelligent, motivated, but inexperienced tribal member who pursues (or sometimes is thrown into) a senior marketing position. This is a true "trial by fire" experience for the trainee, who may receive a little mentoring, but more than likely learns to sink or swim (quickly) on his or her own. This style is characterized by stops and starts with new marketing programs (depending on who is in the marketing exec's ear — GM, tribal council, ad agency, etc.) and a tendency to get everything done at the last minute with very little long-term planning or organization.

The 'account exec' — As many casinos have popped up in cities that previously did not have gaming, oftentimes the only nearby "marketing" resource has been the local ad agency. In many cases, a casino's marketing director may have previously been the account exec for its ad agency. This person is usually organized, intelligent and productive but tends to believe that advertising equals marketing, so he usually has a huge, multi-faceted advertising budget, often to the exclusion of direct mail or players club promotions.

The 'front liner' — This is the casino employee who worked in other departments and then somehow landed in marketing, often through the players club or host areas. She actually understands the gaming business and the importance of connecting with employees and customers, but unless she has a great mentor or some significant quality training, she will have a hard time overcoming her roots to achieve her full marketing growth potential.

The 'fuzzy faced college kid' — Especially in some of the larger casino companies, this is the young recruit with the advanced marketing degree. He is extremely comfortable with technology and is very well versed in the latest, high-powered marketing techniques. But he tends to not understand the everyday gambler (he doesn't gamble himself and thinks the act of gambling is "stupid") and has a hard time learning to interact with a casino's lifeblood — its frontline employees.

I'm sure there may be other "marketing styles" and many individuals may not cleanly fall into any single category. But what's it all mean?

Simply put, I think most marketing execs (or any gaming execs for that matter) come to the party with significant "gaps in their game." The issue is not how you got there, but how you are going to leverage this tremendously important marketing role and use it to add ultimate value to the casino. And from my experience, that takes a customer focus, an understanding of the complex, integrated nature of marketing, an analytical eye, relationship-building skills and a willingness to work your tail off around effective marketing principles. If you can do all this, no matter what your starting style, you can achieve the rarest marketing style of all — the "*highly effective marketing pro.*"

The 10 biggest casino marketing sins

Often in my work, I get to do "get everyone on the same page" casino marketing presentations. Typically many of client casinos' senior executives (from all departments) are in the room to hear me speak and (hopefully) participate in the discussion that this presentation always seems to generate.

Anyway, in this "customer-focused marketing" presentation, I try to make a few key points:

- That "marketing" should not be a department, but rather an integrated way of doing business involving all departments (you should see the looks I sometimes get from the operations guys and gals on that one);

- You need to focus on the 20 percent of your gaming customers that typically account for 80 percent of your profits;

- A player's "lifetime worth" is a much better strategic focus than their average daily theoretical worth *today*;

- Information and a player's likelihood of being "a gamer" are two critical marketing variables and marketing plans can be constructed around them in a highly-prioritized fashion; and

- Some marketing tactics are better than others and yes, there are ways to effectively compare them.

I always try to close my presentations with some fun and effective ways to leave participants with some useful takeaways and some bite-size chunks of marketing magic that they can hang on their wall or refer to in their notes. And that's how I created a closing summary, based on the aforementioned principles, of *how not to* do effective casino marketing. I call it "The 10 Biggest Casino Marketing Sins" that I have seen." I share them with you now, in reverse order (a' la David Letterman) along with a brief description of what I mean:

The 10 biggest casino marketing sins:

10. *Trying to be who you aren't* — This is the Las Vegas Strip casino trying to attract locals (and the Las Vegas locals casino trying to attract Strip customers). It's the terribly remote tribal casino trying to be a regional entertainment center or a destination resort. It's the struggling megaresort with a weak stomach for taking big bets fancying itself as a high-roller haven. This is any casino, in a desperate attempt to grab more business, that positions itself as something it can't possibly be.

9. *Chasing unqualified groups and lists* — In this sinful activity, casinos adopt the short-sighted attitude that, "Hey, our current customers already love us, we need new customers!" They buy prospecting lists, do expensive advertising in outer markets and bring in any groups they can find to fill their hotel rooms. They forget that it's easier and more efficient to get your current customers to spend a little more or stay a little longer than it is to milk that mythical "untapped market."

8. *Short-term marketing focus* — This sin typically involves a casino looking out to next week or next month and saying, "Hey, business looks weak, let's do something!" It's reaction rather than proactive and reasoned strategic marketing.

7. *Half-assed measurement* — Sometimes this involves no measurement at all, but it absolutely includes every instance where a casino spends money to drive business and doesn't know "reasonably" to "absolutely" well what its return on investment was ("What was the cost per response of that ad campaign???").

6. *Advertising is a sacred cow* — In this sin it typically means that advertising is a disproportionate (and often bloated) part of the casino budget. But hey, don't touch it; the GM (or the tribal chairperson, or the CEO or the marketing VP) feels we need to be "top of mind."

5. *Always looking for the home run* — In this sin, simple, solid and tried and true isn't enough. We need "sexy" and "flashy" and "more of Las Vegas." So roll out the Mercedes, ramp up the $1 million giveaway and get the big names in the showroom (usually on a crowded Saturday night)!

4. *Taking current customers for granted* — This sin is manifested in many ways, but let me tell you about this in the words of your own customers: "Hey, we play here four times a week and rarely get anything. But a bus rolls up and these strangers get a roll of quarters, a free meal and a gift (and then they clog up my favorite machines!). What about me???"

3. *Viewing marketing as a "department"* — In this sin, you typically hear operators talk about "those marketing people" and marketing people saying, "We bring 'em in, and *their* frontline employees run 'em off." This is the sin of not understanding, or not believing, that every employee needs to be a marketer.

2. *Lack of a marketing plan* — In this sin, I don't mean "budgets" or "goals" or a tweak of last year's marketing schedule. No, I'm referring to a true strategic marketing plan, created by *all* of a property's senior executives, based on effective marketing principles and real marketing needs. It's a sin that few casinos have this.

1. *Listening to the GM instead of the customers* — In this most mortal sin of all, the trademarks are a cavalier GM (or tribal council chairperson or marketing exec) who makes marketing decisions based on what *he* or *she* thinks is best, or most profitable or "what we really need around here." It's often characterized by a lack of listening to customers, executives spending little or no time on the casino floor and department heads managing to rules, budgets and the GM — to anything and anyone, but the casino customer.

And there you have my top 10 casino marketing sins. And if you are a sinner, fear not, it is never too late to go and beg your customers for forgiveness and to ensure that those who giveth don't taketh away.

You know you're a real casino marketer if...

Being a consultant is extremely gratifying. To watch gaming clients make fundamental changes in how they approach their marketing process and then see them increase gaming revenues, reduce marketing costs or improve guests' satisfaction (hopefully accomplishing all three!), well that is one heck of a professional rush. For me, this gratification is especially heightened in the Indian gaming world, where improved marketing success has such tangible payoffs not only at the casino operational level, but often at the casino executive level and the community level as the fruits of learning cascade through the organization.

But certainly, gaming marketing consulting has its own unique set of challenges that need to be overcome to experience this deep sense of gratification (hey if it was always easy, anyone could do it!). Sometimes these challenges involve people, sometimes organizations, sometimes technology, sometimes it's the marketing culture (or the lack of it), sometimes, yes, it's politics.

But I believe the biggest challenge in achieving casino marketing consulting success is that most casino management teams do not have a common understanding of what marketing is. Some casino executives believe marketing equals advertising. Others, (especially CFO types) believe it is a nebulous expense that needs to be controlled at all times or it will spiral out of control. Others believe it is big-time casino promotions, or TV advertising or big name entertainers on weekends.

Rarely do you see an entire casino management team dedicated to the common proposition that: *marketing is an integrated approach to doing business, involving all members of the organization, focusing on the three constituencies of customers, employees and communities.*

But rather than trying to wax eloquently on what casino marketing really is or build further on this philosophical model, I thought it would be best to bring it to the tangible, personal level with the wish that you might know great casino marketing when you see it, at least in yourself. So with apologies to Jeff Foxworthy, I would like to share with you the following:

You know you're a real casino marketer if...

- You spend more time with customers and employees than you do with meetings and paperwork;

- You know your top 100 customers by name and make it a point to talk with each of them at least once a year;

- You wear the same silly promotional buttons that you ask your frontline employees to wear;

- You are a member of at least one community organization in the city or area where your casino does business;

- You routinely eat your lunch in the employee dining room;

- You have a healthy skepticism of most coupon, busing and freebie programs;

- The customer service you give your employees and customers is a model for others;

- Your list of unreturned phone calls never has any names on it;

- Your casino really has a marketing plan and you were a part of building it;

- You would sit in the dunk tank at the employee picnic;

- You routinely work on Saturdays;

- You park your car where all of the other employees park theirs;

- You believe in proformas, post formas and any other "formas" that measure how well your marketing programs are working;

- You can navigate your casino's player tracking system and find pertinent information on your players;

- You actually worked at least eight hours last year performing the duties of a frontline employee;

- You show up at your casino's VIP events and spend more time talking with casino VIPs than with the other casino executives;

- You have gambled at every one of your competitors' facilities in the past year;

- You know the names of every one of your employees, plus the names of their spouses and children;

- You routinely pick up litter on your casino floor;

- You told at least 100 employees last year what a "great job" they were doing;

- You actually read and understand the marketing budget and rarely get caught up in disagreements about which department should pay for it;

- You can define the word: *Incremental*;

- You believe that prospecting is best left to gold miners;

- Your department has begun to explore the concept of turning your employees into trained salespeople;

- You know in what month Customer Service Week takes place;

- You celebrate Customer Service Week;

- You are known for bringing fun into the casino workplace;

- You took the marketing director to lunch last month;

- You read at least one John Romero book; and

- You asked employees for suggestions then actually listened to them.

Marketing in highly-regulated environments

Gaming is certainly a highly-regulated industry, more regulated than even the nuclear power industry (although as a society, we may have our priorities a little screwed up there). This regulation is certainly a good thing as public confidence in the integrity of our gaming product is critical to our success. If the public couldn't trust the honesty of our games and how we do business, I doubt that we would be successful for very long.

But different aspects of the gaming industry certainly require different levels of regulation. Most would agree that ensuring the integrity of casino games and the full accounting of all casino drops should require strict and clear regulation. Most would also agree that regulating the color of casino carpet would be unnecessary, almost stupid, regulation. Yet no two gaming jurisdictions seem to agree on what should constitute effective regulation of the marketing function for the modern day casino.

I have worked in gaming markets where casinos are not allowed to advertise any aspect of gaming; others where there are no restrictions; still others where the types of gaming advertising allowed is restricted by regulation. Some gaming markets require gaming regulatory approval of *all* casino marketing promotions; others where gaming commission involvement with casino promotions is either limited or non-existent. Casino marketing regulatory schemes certainly run the gamut from being permissive and laissez-faire to being highly-restrictive and almost totalitarian.

As a free-wheeling often "out-of-the-box" marketer who is willing to do almost "whatever it takes" (legally and ethically of course) to drive gaming business, my heart goes out to casino marketers who must labor in the most highly-restrictive, gaming marketing environments. Much of their time is spent getting approvals from regulatory agencies, or doing administrative paperwork or putting together marketing concepts that will pass regulatory muster, yet still be fun and hassle free for casino guests — not always easy things to design effectively. Marketers in other industries do not have to deal with near the amount of regulatory intrusiveness that these casino marketers do and thus are free to spend more time dedicated to growing business. Last I heard, that is what marketers are supposed to do.

My goal is not to get on a soapbox for less marketing regulation in the gaming industry, although a case could probably be made for it. But in other areas, like problem gambling marketing standards, there could probably be better, clearer, more customer-sensitive regulation. So accepting that gaming jurisdictions are what they are and that their rules are unlikely to change dramatically, let's focus on what casino marketers can do to be more effective in these highly-regulated environments. From my experience, working with many of these marketing folks, here are some tips:

Don't whine, accept it. Your gaming commission marketing rules and procedures are not negotiable, they are not going to change appreciably and you will have to deal with them tomorrow, and the day after that and the day after that. Set your mind that it is part of the territory.

Build relationships with individuals in the various gaming regulatory agencies, be they internal, external or both. You'd be surprised how sometimes inflexible systems can suddenly have some flexibility because a marketing manager and a regulatory manager actually can sit down and talk person to person in a reasonable and civil manner. So have coffee with an auditor, state official or gaming commission member.

Get extremely organized and never miss a marketing regulatory deadline. Not only might it jeopardize the successful execution of your marketing event or program, but it will leave a bad taste in regulators' mouths. As marketers, you don't want them feeling that marketing always puts them under the gun by getting their approvals "at the last minute," or "after the fact" or "always late."

Document well and call for help when you need it. Sometimes regulatory agencies do hamper the marketing approval process, perhaps for valid reasons or sometimes just because *they can*. If they are severely hampering your marketing efforts with slow responses or unreasonable demands, keep a record of it and call on help (the GM can be a good ally) when you need to get something unstuck.

Pay special attention to marketing rules and regulations that speak to problem gambling (advertising tag lines, marketing codes of conduct, etc.). This area will only become increasingly more important to jurisdictions and casino marketers. Being ahead of the curve on this issue will not only be the right thing to do, but also win you support from regulatory agencies.

Stay creative and innovative. Just because there are marketing rules, deadlines and prohibited practices, doesn't mean that there aren't some ways that you can legally and ethically "skin the cat." For instance, some jurisdictions do not allow casino loyalty programs based on amount gambled but do allow forms of marketing based on visitation. Find out the acceptable alternatives and pursue them!

Marketing in restrictive gaming markets can be tedious, time consuming and counter-productive. But above all, it is still *necessary* — probably more so than in markets where promotions pop out of the oven and (almost) anything goes.

How to use someone like me

I have had my own consulting company for several years now. It goes without saying that consultants should be individuals or companies that provide real help to organizations. Oftentimes, consulting services carry a price tag that can make tribal chairpersons, general managers or CEOs gulp, especially if the consulting work was not anticipated in the annual budget.

Yes, you can find a consultant for just about every need — there probably is even a consultant who can help you find and manage consultants — and they certainly run the gamut when it comes to levels of experience, expertise and effectiveness.

Given this potentially significant investment in a consultant and the critical need to have him or her be as effective as possible, you owe it to yourself and your organization to maximize the benefits of the consulting relationship. With that in mind, I offer you the following tips on how to use someone like me:

Ask yourself if you really need a consultant — Does the prospective consultant truly offer a perspective, a skill or a service that does not already exist in your organization? Are you sure that you have exhausted all potential sources of assistance in your own company? Are you using a consultant because you just don't want to do the work yourself? Does the desire for a consultant highlight deeper needs or weaknesses in your organization?

Once you have decided to use a consultant, be sure to work with him or her to define the project and the process for accomplishing it — You will have some great thoughts and some lofty expectations regarding the consulting project. So will the consultant. But if you don't sit down and get on the same page together, you run the risk of disappointment. Somewhere between "consultant tells management what to do" and "management tells consultant how to work" is a value-adding collaboration. Do your part in creating it.

Share information with your consultant — If you truly desire a useable, well-conceived consulting project, give your consultant any piece of information that *might* even be helpful in his or her work. If you are slightly paranoid about sharing sensitive company information, either get over it or have the consultant sign a confidentiality agreement.

Make the appropriate people in your organization aware of the consulting project — If possible, even elicit their help in defining the project and the process by which it will work. The last thing you want to do, for example, is to tell your marketing director that you have just hired this great marketing consultant. He or she will feel threatened or unwanted, both of which are undesirable consequences. It is better to get input and buy-in on the front end from key managers.

Stay in touch with your consultant — Things change. Information gets old. Scope of projects can be altered. Surprising results can vary the course of investigation. Important competitive information may call for immediate action. You may realize that you have forgotten something. You may see the opportunity to expand or contract the project. These and many more are good reasons to keep in contact with your consultant during the course of the project. So put your hired gun's phone number on the top of the list of calls to make and calls to return.

Demand ways to do for yourself tomorrow what the consultant does for you today — A good consultant can bring knowledge to organizations. A better consultant helps organizations learn how to gain this knowledge by themselves.

Share the results — Why expend all the time, money and energy on gaining the wisdom that a consultant can bring if that wisdom is not shared with people in the organization who can benefit from it? It is extremely important to make the consultant's work both *known* and *actionable* within the organization.

Pay your consultant in a timely manner — Sure, this sounds simple and even self-serving, but you would be surprised at the amount of time and energy spent by consultants to chase down payment from organizations. This affects the consulting company's cash flow (I know, I know, that's not *your* problem), but more importantly sends a negative message about your company to the gaming community and moves you to a place near the bottom of the consultant's priority list for future projects.

For me, it has been tremendously educational and gratifying to have been a consultant for the past four years, especially in Indian Country, where I feel a tremendous amount of pride and satisfaction in helping Native Americans finally achieve some measure of social and economic justice.

And sure there are things about the consulting world that are frustrating. Some clients don't listen or are too stubborn to be able to help. Extended time on the road can begin to wear you down. Some gaming executives bounce in and out of "consulting" every time they are out of work, giving the whole consulting profession a bad, "fly by night" image.

But the bottom line to best use "someone like me" is to remember that we often-disparaged consultants are just like you. We love this gaming business, just like you.

And for someone like me to succeed, I need you and your organization to succeed. When we both can do that, and when we can also truly feel a part of a team, if only for a brief time, then we will have created value not only for our respective companies and their customers, but also for ourselves.

Why I love Harrah's

I have not been known to gush too often in talking or writing about casino properties or companies. It's not that I haven't been impressed at times. MGM Mirage has some great facilities, as does Mohegan Sun, Agua Caliente and Sandia. Isle of Capri Casinos, Boyd Gaming, Barona and the Mill Casino have wonderful employee cultures. The Horseshoe (everywhere but Las Vegas) is a great pure gambling experience. Seven Feathers is dramatically altering guest expectations of the Indian gaming experience. Yes, there is some good stuff going on out there.

It's just that, in my opinion, no casino has the entire package, the whole enchilada, the top to bottom *real deal*.

Except for Harrah's.

Now, I have to confess that earlier in my career, I worked for Harrah's for almost 10 years. But that insider perspective might just as likely make me want to diss them, as praise them.

Truth be told, I liked them then, but I like them even more now.

So why my 15 year love affair with Harrah's? Good question. I have spent a considerable amount of time thinking about that. Here's why:

People and service strategies — While many properties and companies talk about their people and their service, Harrah's *does it!* It has a proprietary diagnostic tool (The Better People Inventory) that helps it identify the "Harrah's type" of service-oriented individual. It does a ton of service training (People Pledged to Excellence). It rewards *all* employees, in part at least, for quarterly customer service scores. It has a terrific management development program (Excellence in Management). To top it all off, Harrah's even hired a Harvard customer service guru (Gary Loveman) to run the entire company!

Technology — Major casino companies are just now figuring out how to link their multiple player reward programs into one. Harrah's has been doing it for years. Casino hotels talk about yield managing their hotels. Harrah's has sophisticated software programs that actually (and efficiently) do that. Most casinos have Web sites as window dressing. Harrah's Web site grows its business and creates business opportunities.

Research — Most casinos' "research" is some cheesy comment card program. Harrah's has extensive, coordinated efforts to talk to its important customers *and stay* on top of important society and industry trends that might impact the gaming business.

Thinking outside the box — While many casino companies were spending money and working hard politically to defeat Indian gaming initiatives, Harrah's stayed out of the fray and instead built close relationships and developed numerous opportunities in Indian Country. When the industry had its head buried in the sand on the problem gambling issue, Harrah's developed a sincere response to the dilemma along with cutting-edge programs. When high-end Las Vegas casinos were chasing expensive and unprofitable high-end business, Harrah's Rio property got out of that game. Whether it's been investments in airlines, innovative cooperative ventures or aggressive but value-adding mergers, Harrah's is always ahead of the curve.

Marketing strategy — Harrah's clearly understands the three marketing pillars of customers, employees and communities. It focuses on the right marketing tactics — its database marketing is the best in the business. Its promotions and rewards focus on the players who spend their dollars with Harrah's. In short, Harrah's is the greatest single example of the success of the service profit chain and it has become a true marketing company.

Phil Satre — I don't know how or why Harrah's CEO got his powerful customer and employee perspective, but the rest of the senior industry execs should take a page out of his book. And oh yeah, a front-line employee feels comfortable in approaching Phil … and vice versa. Now there's a lesson!

Yes, I confess, I love Harrah's. Are they perfect? Not by a long shot. Its insularity can make it miss new ideas. Its top executives still leak away to other companies. Its once "warm and cozy nest" has much more of a hard-nosed business edge about it. It still grapples with design and with food product. Its senior executives (with the wonderful customer focus) need to spend more time with customers.

But that's all small potatoes. By far, Harrah's is the best in the business. You can learn a lot from them. I know I already have.

Pearls of wisdom

Marketing can be a very humbling profession. Great promotions can sink in the tide of a "soft market." Great ideas can turn into stupid ideas with a single, unanticipated consequence. Customers might not only take the "hook," they might take the entire fishing pole as well.

Yes, in the marketing game it's hard to really "know" anything. The best you can hope for is having extended moments of strongly suspected truths. Then everything changes and you don't know anything ... again.

Yet since most marketing people feel that they know just about everything, I thought I'd share what I feel I knew (I just realized these). I strongly suspect they're true. But they might not be. Or it might be true just for me.

What I know:

- There is no better communication network than the pipeline among vendors who have discovered you need 10,000 key chains;

- Direct mail to Canada will get screwed up no matter what you do;

- Successful marketing promotions are conceived on totally different neural pathways in the brain;

- No one understands the psyche of a slot player, including a slot player;

- Anything longer than one sentence to describe a strategic marketing plan is needless hype;

- Providing cocktail service to gamers instantaneously, through IVs, still wouldn't be quick enough;

- The game of craps is the biggest missed marketing opportunity in the casino business;

- Slot players don't want a cash back program. They want their cash back from yesterday;

- Slot players do want "time on device" and no one knows how to give it to them;

- There is a good-sized market for "noisy, smoky, dirty, crowded;"

- A casino floor needs a path through it that fits the concept of *explore and reward;*

- Casino employees should all be professional entertainers who love to gamble;

- The anti-casino lobby doesn't understand that most people like to bet on something;

- The most powerful person in a casino is a dealer;

- Nobody has figured out direct marketing yet;

- Casino customers should get treated commensurate with their potential lifetime worth, not their average bet today;

- The fact that few casino executives gamble is probably a bad thing;

- The next table game with mass appeal will be created within five years by someone from outside the casino industry;

- Every casino executive should be required to spend at least 20 percent of his or her time being a casino customer;

- The Big 6 Wheel will get more play if you let the customers spin the wheel;

- Your own casino employees are your single most neglected form of competitive customer research;

- Bob Stupak's classic article on "zings and stings" (*Gambling Times*, circa 1980) should be required reading for all casino marketers;

- Smart casino gamblers are smarter than smart casino executives;

- You have to admire what the Native American communities have been able to accomplish with gaming;

- You can know when to market on the Internet by knowing if your slot players have computers;

- A casino's executive management team should do all of the hiring and orientation of employees;

- The best kept secret for educating up and coming casino executives is the University of Nevada Reno's Executive Development Program;

- The best casino operators spend a lot of time on the casino floor, talking with employees and customers;

- The first casino company to successfully implement the Nordstrom way of doing business will be a huge success;

- There is a tremendously powerful lesson in the Stratosphere's recent marketing experiment;

- Harold Smith, Bill Harrah, Benny Binion and Steve Wynn discovered it, and everyone else screws it up;

- Casino executives are incredibly ignorant about casino mathematics;

- You will never see a program like the Harrah's Institute again;

- Instead of trying to peddle "single 0" roulette, American casino operators should just increase the paybacks on the "double 0" game;

- It is possible to learn more dealing craps than attending Stanford;

- The most interesting day I can think of would be to spend 24 hours in a room with Glenn Schaeffer and Phil Satre; and

- Marketing columnists all share a deep need to be listened to by their mothers and fathers.

What's the number? What's the number?

I have had many requests in the past year from beleaguered casino operators who want a simple benchmark and an industry comparison figure in order to evaluate if they are in line with their marketing expenditures.

The question usually gets asked as, "What's the number?" meaning, "What percentage of my casino revenues should I be spending on marketing?"

I always get nervous hearing that question because I know the answer is essentially meaningless.

Sure, I could gather marketing budgets from Casino X, Casino Y and Casino Z and say that, "9 percent is the number," based on their averages.

But here are the problems with such a simplified comparison and attempt at benchmarking marketing expenditures:

All casinos are different. How can you compare a small tribal casino in North Dakota with Foxwoods, for example? The North Dakota casino probably spends some money on advertising, a little on direct mail and perhaps has a few casino promotions. Foxwoods, of course, would have full-blown marketing staffs, extensive player development and every marketing function that you can think of.

Not all casinos have all of the same functions lumped under "marketing," thus comparing associated marketing expenses can be misleading. For instance, some casinos put slot club point redemption expenses under marketing, some put them under the slot department. Some casinos put all advertising expenses to marketing, some allocate it to the various operating departments that utilized it. Comparing casinos that treat marketing expenses differently is truly comparing apples and oranges.

Some casinos have unique initiatives that are called "marketing." For instance, customer service programs have a powerful marketing impact and a few casinos have customer service "stuff" in the marketing budget. But most casinos (if they spend any money on it) put customer service expenses with the human resources department. So when you want to compare marketing expenses, do you count customer service expenditures? Can you discern the expenses buried in HR? See the problem?

Various casinos are in varying competitive situations ranging from a full-blown monopoly to brutal competition. How can you benchmark marketing expenditures between a casino that has to spend a pile of money to stay competitive and one that (essentially) just has to open its doors and count its money? Likewise, a casino that has been open for 10 years and has now achieved pretty complete market awareness is different from one that just opened and needs to spend a lot of money telling people they are *open* (bigger advertising expenses). How can you benchmark marketing expenses for the infant versus the preteen casino?

Casino marketing departments waste a lot of money — especially on advertising — with often no ability to measure return on investment for a certain marketing tactic. So if you wanted to benchmark your marketing expenses, why would you use a bloated industry standard?

It is only natural for casino executives, from both traditional and tribal gaming organizations, to seek a "number" to manage to, whether it be marketing expense as a percentage of revenue or other numbers associated with labor, food costs or hold percentages. But when it comes to that too mystical department called marketing, even if you could address all of the comparison issues raised, it would still be difficult to peg what you should reasonably be spending.

Does that mean you should ignore marketing expenses and give up hope of getting your hands around what are reasonable marketing budgets? Absolutely not! It just means that you have to develop your own number. To do this effectively you have to establish some strong guiding principles like: "Spend the majority of your marketing dollars on the customers who spend their gambling dollars with *you*." You need to focus on player segments that can make the most difference like current un-carded active players or premium inactive players (give them a call!). You need to choose marketing tactics that have a significant measurable return. Above all, you need to make sure that you have some of that marketing largesse spent in finding out what *your* customers want.

Indeed, that should be your marketing charge — *find out what your customers want and give it to them*. It will make your search for the appropriate marketing expense "number" a much easier one. Then you can begin to compare yourself against the most important number of all — how well you are meeting your casino guests' expectations.

The need to win — why people gamble

In my lifetime, I have heard many different theories as to why people like to gamble. Although identifying these causes undoubtedly is a complex and contentious issue, if gaming operators could get their hands around this "gambling urge," it would certainly be valuable for their business.

Some of the speculation I have heard is well known. "It's a temptation like sex and alcohol that morally weak people have trouble avoiding." "It's caused by gaming operators using unscrupulous marketing tactics to prey upon folks" (I love that one). "It's an escape from often difficult, painful or humdrum lives."

Personally, I think these hypotheses on gambling are all misguided BS or the product of people who have agendas to peddle. People gamble because they have a need to win, period. Now, I didn't say that this need was a basic need or even that it was a healthy one. In fact, I believe that this need is symptomatic of a much deeper need and that our competitive, capitalistic society helps to produce it.

By the time most people reach the legal age to gamble, they have competed for grades, for trophies, for peer bragging rights, for parental affection, for friends and lovers, for jobs, for you name it. If you ask these products of our highly-competitive society if they have "won" enough in the course of their lifetime, most would say, "no."

Now enter gambling. Here comes this fast-paced activity that speaks directly to this need to win. Multi-line nickel machines pay out almost every spin. Blackjack allows "winning" almost every other hand. Even slower paced gambling forms, like keno, or bingo or horse racing allow some periodic fulfillment of this need to win.

From my experience, casinos that understand this "need to win" notion (or at least unknowingly cater to it) generally outperform casinos that do not. The Horseshoe casinos in the South and Midwest are all market leaders — not because they are nice facilities (which they are) but because their long-standing liberal gaming proposition is well known and speaks to this "need to win." Other similar examples exist with the Cal Neva in Reno, Bronco Billy's in Cripple Creek, Colo. and Barona Valley Ranch Resort & Casino in Lakeside, Calif. Granted, Barona also exists in a heretofore underserved gaming market, but its "Certified Loose" slots and its focus on liberal table games with big limits has produced a "place to gamble" reputation for Barona, as well as helped blunt the impact of recent competition in the San Diego area.

Likewise, if you look at published monthly gaming statistics from across North America, you will see a very strong correlation between slot volume (high) and slot hold percentage (low). Slot market leaders all tend to have the loosest slots and while cynics might say that a customer cannot tell the difference between a slot hold percentage of 6.41 versus 5.97, I would suggest that not only can they feel the difference (with more frequent wins), but also that this perception brands the looser casino in their minds as "the place to win."

Other casinos can effectively speak to this "need to win" with the use of casino promotions and winning celebrations. The best casino promotions have lots of winners with small- to medium-sized awards like the Station Casinos do in Las Vegas. While cars, boats and big cash giveaways can produce excitement and participation in a cash promotion, lots of smaller prizes produce more winners and speak more effectively to the "need to win." Likewise, when you can enhance the winning that *does* occur in your casino (jackpot announcements, celebrations, winner photos, invitational events for winners, etc.) you directly address this "need to win" principle.

Slot hit frequency is yet another factor in this "winning" formula. You can give your customers $5 on a winning slot pull (for instance) or you can give them five winning pulls of $1 each. Without affecting machine performance, slot customers can be made to feel more like winners. Many casinos use this high-hit frequency tactic.

At one casino where I worked, we conducted an experiment whereby senior executives approached active slot players and asked them to name any one thing that the executive could do for them *right now*. The number one answer was, "Let me win." Not free meals, not more drinks, not less smoke, but simply *let me win*. You will hear this response loud and clear if you ever conduct (and sit in on) customer focus group sessions at your casino.

There is nothing wrong with a casino being known for great service, or great food, or clean facilities or a great players club. But if your casino is not known as a place to *win*, you are missing your customers' greatest need and helping them take a hike to try out your competitors.

We all know that gamblers will likely lose, but if you can maximize and highlight your casino's winning occurrences, you will have created the most powerful marketing formula possible — fulfillment of your guests' need to *win*.

Where to find new casino players

Having worked with over 100 casinos now — many, of course, being Native American casinos — I can tell you that one chronic and recurring issue is where to find more (or new) casino customers. The following are the (mostly ineffective) tactics that I have seen to address this customer development issue:

Greatly expanded casino product — Whether it's more amenities, hotel rooms, golf courses, convention centers, entertainment pavilions, water parks, you name it — this tactic usually tries to expand geographic reach or just give more potential gamers other reasons to visit. The problem is that this tactic can be very expensive and many times the activity is not even linked to the casino. A concertgoer, golfer or conference attendee may not even have to set foot in the casino!

More advertising — This is a real dandy that is usually foisted upon casinos by advertising agencies (of course). Look, most casinos have now been open for several years. Most people within the reach of advertising know you have a casino by now and have made their choice whether to be a patron. So more advertising just preaches to the choir (plus to the 70 percent of the public who will *never* come to your casino — minors, religious folks, anti-gamers, the poor, etc.). Or worse, more advertising needs *more giveaways* to generate more response, cutting into margins and attracting the coupon clipping crowd and lookie-loos.

Test mailing lists — If these lists were any good, do you think they'd be for sale? This tactic is generally peddled by direct marketing firms who will try to impress you with the sheer numbers on their lists as well as the "demographic," "psychographic" or "socio-economic" variables that make their list members likely to be "players." Hey, your best bet is your own list.

New slot product — This tactic can work, especially in situations where already popular machines or innovations (multi-line nickel video games, progressives, hot-branded games, one-cent and two-cent games, etc.) are finally allowed into a gaming jurisdiction. But it's usually not near as strong a tactic as the slot salespeople would lead you to believe.

More extensive casino promotions — Again, this tactic can bring in new players, but typically you are only "bribing" them until the next lucrative giveaway comes along.

Buses — I have seen a few casinos profit from this tactic … but not many. This tactic is seductive because the casino fills up with bodies for a period of time when the buses are on property. But when you factor in the (continuing) costs to pay both the bus company *and* the bus customer, the difficulty in measuring bus group worth and the regular customers run off by the hordes of bus "aliens," this tool typically is a loser.

Initiation, expansion or promotion of bingo — Yes, many bingo players will play slot machines, but remember that these players are first and foremost *bingo players* and how many casinos make money on bingo??? While I respect that many operators, especially Indian gaming tribes, got their start in bingo, this game is dying and people that play it are mostly low-worth players. Get them on a Class II game and fill your bingo hall with penny and nickel multi-line slots!

Steal some hosts with lists — This tactic usually involves hiring "player development professionals" (AKA: unscrupulous hosts with purloined black books). Sure, this can bring you new business … for a while … or until your host takes that list to a competitor for a few thousand dollars more in salary. And oh yeah, a few of "your" customers have a tendency of having worked their way on "his" list. Stay away from this tactic or else get a top-notch lawyer.

Assorted other tactics — Junket reps, sales groups, radio promos, etc., etc., etc. I lump these into the grab bag of well-meaning irrelevance. Some have a little new player development value, but most are relative wastes of time.

So there you have it — a pretty weak bunch of tactics to find or develop new casino players. "So what's a casino to do?" you are probably asking. Let me suggest this:

You see those few hundred people on your casino floor right now? Half of them you probably don't even know. Some of them are visiting a casino for the first time (think it's important that they have a good experience???). Some are customers of your competitors who either got ticked off, lost several times in a row or are just checking you out. Some are *your* customers who would come more often if you found out what they need to do that.

My point is this. In looking for "new" players, you might want to start among your "old" players. You might think you already "own" them, but I guarantee they've got more money to spend with you if you only would show them how. And you can pay for it by stopping most of that other ineffective crap that might keep your marketing folks busy, but does little for your tribal casino's bottom line.

What Harrah's knows that you don't

In my four-plus years of casino marketing consulting, I have worked with over 100 different casinos now. Big casinos, small casinos, government casinos, Indian casinos, well run casinos and dysfunctional casinos.

But I have done very little work for Harrah's Entertainment, even though I previously worked for them for nearly 10 years and have scores of friends and associates still with Harrah's in senior capacities. And although it may sting my consultant's pride, there is a good reason why Harrah's doesn't need to feed at my "expert advice trough."

Quite simply, it doesn't need me ... or anyone else for that matter. You see, Harrah's has figured it out. It knows things that you don't.

Actually, you probably know (or at least strongly suspect to be true) what Harrah's knows. But Harrah's *does it* — consistently, relentlessly and innovatively. Harrah's does the whole ball of wax; everyone else just has bits and pieces of Harrah's winning casino formula.

"But what about MGM Mirage, Horseshoe Gaming, Isle of Capri or Argosy Gaming?" you might ask.

"Mere pretenders to the throne," I would answer. And the same would hold true for other quality casino companies like Boyd Gaming, Ameristar, Park Place and Station Casinos. Or well-run Indian casinos like Barona, Mohegan Sun and Agua Caliente.

You're all playing catch up to Harrah's and I'm going to tell you why. Here's what Harrah's knows that you don't:

What business you are in — Sure, we all now can recite "casino entertainment" in unison, but if you read Harrah's stuff, you will see that it is in the "service and marketing business." Pretty strong stuff.

Where its bread is buttered — Only Harrah's uses the phrase: "Avid Experience Players," its term for that 20 percent of gaming customers who produce 80 percent of a casino's revenues. Certainly other casinos try to cater to this "high end," but Harrah's stays away from "buying the business" of the non-loyal, risky high rollers. It also has created a nifty package of core benefits for its Diamond and Platinum card members ... and not just the standard comps and giveaways, but things that most matter to good gaming customers, like *not having to wait in line* (Harrah's "express" hotel check in, show seating, chip cashing, etc. for Diamond and Platinum members).

How to use technology — While many casino companies have made strides in using technology in what for years has been a techno-phobic business, only Harrah's has made quantum leaps in leveraging computer applications. Witness the awards it has won for its Total Rewards player reward system and for being "one of the best technology companies to work for." Just take a look at its hotel yield management system.

The power of branding — It used to be that Caesars was the most recognizable casino brand name, but no longer — it's Harrah's! And while it did a lot of things to achieve this, Harrah's did one simple and common sense thing that Park Place, MGM Mirage and Mandalay could learn from as they try to drive cross visitation among their own properties — Harrah's casinos all have the same name!

Effective use of direct mail — Yes, there are some casinos that are pretty good at direct mail application, but Harrah's has it down to a science (read the article "Welcome to Harrah's" by Joe Ashbrook Nickell on the Internet). It did this by going out and hiring some of the sharpest direct marketing minds in the business *from outside of gaming*. That is another Harrah's strength — its willingness to hire brainpower from other industries.

The people side of the equation — Harrah's knows that the gaming business is not about machines and tables and food and rooms, but about people. This is the heart of its success. Its employees are chosen by a proprietary diagnostic tool that pinpoints the "Harrah's personality." They are trained in programs with acronyms (and effectiveness) unique to Harrah's (P.P.E. — People Pledged to Excellence; E.I.M. — Excellence in Management; E.I.L. — Excellence in Leadership, etc., etc.). Harrah's hires seasoned MBA students for management positions through its President's Associate program. It has the top employee appearance standard through its "Personal Best" program. Even Harrah's dishwashers can earn up to $1,200 in yearly bonuses for achieving a number of goals, including excellence in the TPSS (another Harrah's acronym standing for "Target Patron Satisfaction Survey") — a regular service quality assessment from Harrah's best customers. Yes, Harrah's knows the power of the "service profit chain" and the role of people in it. It even hired a Harvard guru (Gary Loveman) to execute it. A Harvard professor running a casino company? Only at Harrah's!

Before you accuse me of having been brainwashed by my 10 years with Harrah's, let me just say that I know it is not perfect. It grapples with deal making and politics. Its food product, while improved, is inconsistent across the brand. It will never be accused of having superior casino design. Its branded casino promotions are a snore, at least given that they are for Harrah's best customers. Its talented managers continue to leak away to the competition.

But what Harrah's knows that you don't is that this wonderful thing we call "gaming" is the purest example of what should be a customer-focused business. But somewhere in our budgets and regulations and hold percentages and database segmentations and organizational charts and marketing plans, we have forgotten what is truly important.

But Harrah's hasn't, and that is why it knows more than you, why it doesn't need me and why it is everything that should make us all proud to be in the gaming biz.

Rethinking casino organization

When my wife and I were much, much younger (OK, she is *still* young), we worked at a couple of casinos in Laughlin, Nev., when Laughlin was a tiny little resort town (the two main casinos had about 200 slot machines each and the third only got any real business on weekends). Anyway, one of Becky's "jobs" at the smallest casino was being a slot change person for two days a week, a keno writer for two days a week and a cocktail server for one (much more lucrative) day a week. Yes, she was a real utility infielder!

For this small casino, my wife's multiple job roles made a lot of sense. It didn't have a lot of business and what business it had came primarily on weekends. So it cobbled together a full time role for her. Sound familiar? The same dichotomy of weekday/weekend business held true in 1975 and continues to be true for tribal casinos in 2003. Yes, most casino business in any given week occurs in a 48-hour period from Friday evening to Sunday evening.

Of course this creates staffing issues. You need a lot of employees on weekends and only a fraction of that number on weekdays. And on top of that, most employees nag to be off on weekends and, of course, most senior casino executives rarely are seen on weekends. Why aren't our casinos organized around the flow of business and cognizant of the fact that we get slammed on weekends? I dunno, but it's probably linked to "the way we've always done business around here."

Over the years, I have seen some attempts at innovation in casino organization to address these issues: Bar backs fill in occasionally as bartenders. It is fairly common for dealers to work as box persons or floor persons (dual rate). I saw one innovative attempt years ago where a "gaming host" position was created combining the roles of dealer and change person, with employees working a number of days a week in each role. Wow, a breaking of the bounds between slots and table games! But most of this experimentation has been incremental, not revolutionary.

I have heard all the reasons why such a dramatic change in casino organization and job descriptions *cannot* occur: unions, tribal gaming commissions, not enough experienced managers to oversee the new structure, NIGC regulations, internal controls, upsetting employees. In my opinion, these are all excuses. The main reason we do not have a casino organization that really reflects the unique demands and complexities of our casino business is that we haven't yet taken the trouble to create it. Period!

And while I'm not suggesting that you can have a casino organization next week where the same employee serves drinks, deals cards, fixes machines and makes change (but "why not?" I would ask), there are several concrete steps that you *can* take at your tribal casino to enhance productivity with more effective organization and scheduling. Such as:

Vigorously pursue 10 hour (or even 12 hour) workdays for many of your employees. They'll love it, you'll love it and it will get you more hands on deck on weekends.

Look for every opportunity where an employee can work multiple roles within a single department. There is no good reason why a food and beverage employee can't be a cocktail server, a bar back, a bartender, a food server, a host person or even a supervisor — they all involve taking care of customers, don't they?

Make every single senior executive work on Saturday. They'll hate it at first, but hey, *that's when you have all your business!*

Leverage your senior executives across multiple areas. With a little training, there is no reason why a table games manager cannot also oversee bingo, keno, pull tabs, even slots. I realize that "tribal employment opportunities" is often a valid goal with Indian gaming, but you can still have numerous executives in training at lesser, yet still expanded roles.

Sit down with your gaming commission. Explain your goals with an innovative gaming organization and ask for their help in getting there. You may be surprised how they can help you do something if you ask. Otherwise, they may just give you all the myriad of reasons why you *can't.*

Reward your employees for what you want them to do. Learning multiple job roles or working 12 hour shifts should have a clear benefit for them. After all, it has a clear benefit to your Indian casino, doesn't it?

While it would be nice if every employee viewed his or her role as, "just please the guest," exploring innovation in your tribal casino organization can help you come closer to making that simple and powerful goal a reality.

Strategically thinking about bingo

If you are in the gaming business then you likely fit into one of three categories:

- You are a *bingo-only* operation;

- You are a gaming operation *without bingo*; or

- You are a gaming operation that also *has bingo*.

While I do not claim a lot of experience with bingo marketing, many of our clients do have bingo games, so I have become somewhat familiar with many of the issues surrounding this longstanding game of chance. *Bingo only* operations have a hard time competing with casinos. Casinos *with bingo* have a hard time justifying the expenses and floor space associated with a game that more often than not loses money. Casinos *without bingo* either totally ignore any bingo marketing possibilities or tend to grapple with a framework for successfully using bingo, often starting it and stopping its operation on seeming whims. So from my experience, here are some strategic suggestions for the game of bingo, based on your type of gaming operation:

Bingo-only operations:

Unless you have a significant monopoly, driving incremental bingo revenue is quite a challenge for you. As if you didn't know it, you need to carefully control your costs of operation.

Since money is tight, you need to be a creative and innovative marketer, often in guerilla-type fashion. "Must-go" games, big jackpots, theme nights, specialty bingo games, bounce backs, early birds — these tricks and more need to be part of your marketing arsenal.

Since most of your customers are bingo regulars, the customer service and sales ability of your bingo employees needs to be better than outstanding. They should see their jobs not as selling bingo packs, but as *building relationships*!

You likely have a challenge introducing new, younger players to the game of *bingo*. You need to attack this challenge with vigor and *do whatever it takes* to accomplish this introductory marketing to fresh blood.

Your competition can be your friend. If there are other bingo operators, casinos, charity night operators, racetracks or other gaming providers near your area, you need to find ways to work together in some fashion. You can't afford not to.

Casinos with bingo:

Your challenge is often one of being appreciated in a larger (and more profitable) operation. You need to do everything you can to expose and trumpet the true value of bingo to your overall casino operation.

Everyone knows that your bingo players also play slots but you must always try to answer the questions, "How much?" and "Would they still play slots if we didn't have bingo?" And tracking, statistical, even *observational* data helps you make your case.

You need to embrace technology and what it can do for your bingo operation. Electronic bingo, Class II slot games within the bingo room, devices that are half electronic bingo games and half video gaming devices, multi-site linked bingo games, perhaps even Internet bingo — these all hold potential and should be explored.

You need to be a good partner with the rest of your casino. That means making room for more one-cent slot machines in your bingo space, using your bingo room for multipurpose, revenue-generating activity (entertainment, meeting space, etc.) and *generally showing your slot and table game executives how bingo operations could augment their profits.*

Casinos without bingo:

While you might not understand how bingo fits in your faster-paced casino environment, you need to be open to the idea of using bingo as a traffic driver or an additional gaming amenity. Check out how the Sands Regency in Reno added bingo as a component of a locals strategy with its "B-1 With Sands Bingo" campaign.

You might see opportunity using bingo as a special event or as a VIP party as it is an activity that most casino gamers understand and after all, it *is* a form of gaming. Check on all regulation issues involved in using bingo on an intermittent basis.

If you are a Class III tribal casino without bingo, you might check out how "bingo based slot machines" (Class II) might benefit your gaming operation without impacting your compact rules.

There are slot machines that look like bingo (Slotto, etc.), casinos have had some luck using bingo as a base for promotions ("fill out this bingo card each time you hit a $100 slot bonus") and partnerships with local bingo operators can be a "win-win" for a casino. Keep on the lookout for these bingo opportunities that can tap into bingo/slot players from the nearby universe of gamers.

Bingo may seem like a slow, dying game with limited revenue opportunity, but it still has a large core player base and is held in high esteem at many tribal casinos where bingo often is the cornerstone of the tribe's gaming success. Many of the tribal members are still avid bingo players. Treat bingo as a marketing opportunity and it will be one!

The strongest casino positioning of all

Probably the biggest single factor in determining the degree to which a casino property will be successful is its long-term positioning. "Positioning" is a broad term that includes the type of physical structure, the marketing strategy, the target customer, the gambling products and their odds, the employees and a variety of other features that define a casino's personality or *who* or *what* it wants to be over time.

Now, I haven't been to all of the North American casinos, whether Indian or non-Indian, but I feel qualified to offer the following observations. It's kind of like, if you work in enough supermarkets you begin to figure out how shelves are filled (rip offs at eye-level, impulse items at check-out, etc.) and what different customers see in different stores, all having essentially the same stuff.

Anyway, as I see it, there are currently five major positionings for North American casino properties:

1. The highly-themed, mega-resort "experience" — This is the newest, most expensive and potentially one of the most effective casino positionings — the modern casino resort. It contains attractions, entertainment, shopping, gambling, amenities. Why, it's a freaking city! And now they are even starting to take on the names of cities — New York-New York, Monte Carlo, Bellagio, Paris. My suggestion to San Francisco, Bora Bora and Rome would be to at least make a few bucks from the deal.

The mega-resort positioning is expensive, and getting more expensive all the time. The advantages of this strategy — if executed properly — are that it opens up major revenue opportunities in the hotel, retail operations and entertainment/attractions areas. It attracts patrons from nearby casino hotels. It hits a wide range of customers. It dwarfs competitors. It is hard to duplicate.

The disadvantages of the mega-resort positioning are few but significant. Wrong themes can be chosen. When done incorrectly (as author David Kranes might say), they might tell a story that people do not want to read. The next, greater, more interesting mega-resort could make all others obsolete. However, in sum, this is an extremely powerful casino positioning that more Indian casinos are starting to explore as they grow.

2. The customer service kings — There are some casino properties, even companies that would like to think that their positioning is based on service and their employees' ability to deliver it. Now, I'm not saying that some casino properties do not provide better service than others, but my belief is that there are few discernible differences in service levels at casino hotels in North America and currently this is not a basis for competitive advantage and thus a weak positioning. I have several theories why casino customer service is poor, but suffice it to say, there ain't no Nordstrom's yet. And the first Indian gaming company to figure it out will have one of the most powerful and potentially enduring positioning of all.

3. The pure gambling joint — A few casinos, most notably the Horseshoe in Las Vegas and the Cal Neva in Reno, have positionings related to the gambling proposition. They are the places to *gamble* — loose slot machines, liberal table game conditions like 10X odds or single-deck blackjack, few, if any, hotel rooms (don't need the hassle or the image of actually being a *hotel*, yuck!), inexpensive food (leaves more money for gambling!), etc.

This is a very powerful positioning when executed properly. It attracts people with a willingness to spend more or to fulfill their fantasy of being a 'gambler' or just being around gamblers. It allows a casino to get away with a lack of attractions, themes or amenities. It focuses on the most profitable part of the business. It gains forgiveness if the property is a little smoky, crowded, dirty or worn — in fact, it almost thrives on it. On the downside, many new recreational gamers find the "gambling joint" unattractive, the games and slots tend to win at a slower pace with greater swings of luck (sounds good to me) and profitable areas of business (hotel, retail, amusements, etc.) are usually missed. This positioning is very strong, however, especially if adhered to fervently, but it is not currently in vogue in Indian Country.

4. The hodgepodge — This is by far the most prevalent casino positioning of all. The "hodgepodge" has a little bit of a theme, a little focus on customer service, a little emphasis on the gambling proposition. Changes in positioning typically involve shuffling the hodgepodge. One general manager tries to get friendly employees, the next tries to target gamblers, the next wants to change the theme and feel. The next tries to do all three.

These properties are for a variety of reasons, severely challenged. If it were possible (and affordable), they would be better served to choose one hanger on which to hang their hat, one consistent message over time that reverberates with more of their type of customer. Is this easy to do? About as easy as turning my Pomeranian into an attack dog.

5. The strongest casino positioning of all — This is easy. It's the fascinating, mega-themed resort with the knock-your-eyeballs out service and the best possible gaming conditions — the hodgepodge turned powerful blend. And no, it doesn't exist. Not even close. But there is a model. It's called Disneyland. Last I heard it was doing OK. Your Indian casino could learn from it.

Promotions

Someone who understands table game marketing

As a former table game executive and a frequent table game player, I have to admit that I have been deeply disappointed in the quality (and quantity) of table game marketing in the gaming industry today. I find it hard to believe the extent to which table game executives have stood back and allowed the ubiquitous slot machine to gobble up casino floor space like Ms. Pac-Man.

So sure, there are some positive signs, such as poker being hot and Gen Y appearing to be a generation of table game players. And yes, a few new table games like Let It Ride, Three Card Poker and Rapid Roulette (a slot product knock-off!) have had some traction in recent years, but the table game product (blackjack, craps and roulette, essentially) and table game marketing have remained very much the same and incredibly resistant to change over the last few decades.

Here is what I see from my vantage point:

A "new game" culture that is extremely resistant to try new games unless they have already proven to be popular (hey, the slot guys and gals slap games on the floor at a dizzying pace and just yank 'em out if they are not performing!).

A focus on regulations and procedures to the detriment of the player experience (for instance, casino dealers can call out "change $100" or check for counterfeit bills 100 percent of the time, but welcome a new player to the game effectively about 50 percent of the time and "sell" the players club card about 20 percent of the time).

Current table game promotions are mainly silly bonuses, coupons or drawings that typically slow down the speed of the game and put a frown on the faces of the dealers.

Table game customer service is mediocre at best, with every happy, motivated and relationship-making dealer (the "game builders") cancelled out by a frowning sourpuss ("game killers").

Current "innovation" in table games involves mainly finding ways for unsuspecting table game players to make "higher-holding" bets on "higher holding" games (a dangerous short-term approach).

But I have discovered one individual, one lone wolf crying out in the desert, who is making a huge difference in casino table games with true innovation, working against a mindset of, "you can't do that" or, "that will never work." His name is Rick Hudson and he is a real table game marketer who routinely makes huge and measurable differences for his clients. And you need to hear about his table game marketing approach unless, of course, you are just fine with slot machines taking over the world.

Rick Hudson is a table game consultant and could be fairly called an odd duck in the gaming industry. He is a former academic (with a degree in organizational development or some such high-brow discipline) who fell into the gaming business by first dealing at the sawdust joints of downtown Las Vegas. He endured many of the dinosaurs in the table game executive world who would "sweat the money" and try to run off table game players who were winning. But besides being a smart guy, Rick was lucky enough to have an enlightened mentor who suggested he should treat winning gamblers as having been given a temporary loan and, "if you are real nice to them, you will get it back with (substantial) interest."

Rick Hudson has been consulting now for several years and has pioneered an integrated concept called Blackjack Happy Hour, which involves random table game promotions. And what is that? Essentially it is a strategic tinkering of the rules or outcomes of the table game betting experience (think random slot bonuses) to create surprise (and gaming value) for the table game customers. The dice "seven out" on the craps table and everyone loses? No problem, just call a "random table game promotion" and the losing roll doesn't count. Or how about paying two to one on blackjack hands for an hour? Or allowing blackjack players to discard their first card in a hand if they don't like it? Or if the "0" or "00" comes up on the roulette wheel, making everyone a winner? There are as many random bonuses as a creative table game manager's mind can come up with.

What has really impressed me with Rick Hudson's Blackjack Happy Hour and its random promotions have been the results — he routinely produces table game revenue increases of 30 percent to 60 percent for clients with an amazingly simple process. A casino chooses a package of surprise rule changes and game outcome alterations (all of which give a big, temporary advantage to the players), rolls it out to its table game customers with great fanfare (and great expense) and then has it settle into its table game culture as a series of surprise bonuses.

You would think it would be easy for Rick Hudson to sell common 50 percent increases in table game revenues to table game operators. But he almost has to fight every step of the way to the bank. Regulators and gaming commission have to buy in. Dealers must become friendlier and create the celebratory mood demanded by random bonus occurrences. Table game managers must loosen up. Advantage players must be backed off as the program is designed for loyal players, not opportunists. Detailed rules and procedures must be created.

But when it all comes together, and so far it always has, Rick Hudson's Blackjack Happy Hour and random table game promotions produce happier customers and more revenue for table game operators. And that is an uncommonly terrific marketing result.

The current state of casino promotions

If there is one thing that casinos do *a lot* of (besides advertising), it's promotions. There are VIP promotions, players club promotions, tournament promotions, food promotions, hotel promotions, slot promotions, table game promotions and entertainment promotions. You'll see bounce-backs, sweepstakes, "swipe and wins," hot seats, bonus cash, sign-up incentives, comps, cash back, drawings, giveaways and mystery jackpots. Yes, casinos have taken the art of promotions to unparalleled heights (some might say "depths"). Never has one industry spent so much on such a promotional artillery.

I certainly do believe that casinos need an effective package of casino promotions and there are valid strategic reasons for conducting them. Certainly casino promotions can be used as a hook to drive property trial. They can increase player retention, whether that measurement be as a "share of wallet" or in extended gaming time. They certainly can increase play of casino VIPs, if the promotion adequately hits their hot buttons. Promotions can also drive off-peak gaming activity, build customer loyalty, increase players club memberships, help meet a competitive threat, reactivate a lapsed player, build employee buy-in, enhance community relations, generate brand awareness and help leverage co-op marketing dollars of various casino marketing partners (soft drink companies, beer vendors, slot manufacturers, etc.).

Wow, casino promotions sound like the ultimate tonic for all that ails a casino!

But based on my extensive work in Casino Land over the years, the "casino promotion reality" that I have seen is much different. So with no ill will intended and with apologies to those casinos who do use casino promotions profitably and strategically, allow me to share my opinions on the current state of casino promotions in North America:

Casino promotions are often too expensive. Sometimes this is a result of "one-upmanship" among casinos in competitive markets. Sometimes this happens because a casino originally overinvested in a promotion and is afraid of cutting back on subsequent editions for fear of customer backlash. Sometimes this is a result of poor (or no) analysis. Whatever the reason, I believe that most casinos greatly overspend on their casino promotions.

Casino promotions unnecessarily overlap in many instances. This usually starts innocently enough. The slot director wants to pump up mid-week business with a hot seat promotion. But then the hotel exec wants to fill some rooms so a discounted (or free) room offer goes out to the casino database. Then business goes soft for a month and the GM wants to offer double slot club points. And then ... you get the picture. Pretty soon the discounts have discounts and things are freer than free (ask an "advantage player" how they exploit this overlapping promotional largesse).

Casino promotions typically are not very exciting. Well, they're meant to be exciting, but usually staff is not skilled or trained as "fun-meisters" or somewhere around the 60th day of the promo, folks are getting a little tired of the (same old) hoopla.

Casino promotions are usually selected with little or no input from customers and sometimes customers are given promotional prizes that they do not want or value. This is usually manifested in the Corvette giveaway at the rural casino with mainly senior gaming customers. Or in the $100,000 grand prize giveaway when customers would prefer 1,000 prizes of $100 each. This disconnect can be avoided by one very simple tactic — ask your customers what they want, and give it to them.

Casino promotions generally have little understanding and in-volvement from frontline casino employees and little participation from senior casino executives. The acid tests here for your casino are simple. If a customer asks one of your employees about an ongoing promotion and gets a glazed look and an, "I dunno" or they vaguely point towards the players club area, your promotional machine is probably not well oiled. And if your senior execs only want to see financial results from the promotion and not want to laugh and scratch with customers at the promotion, your casino is likely missing the boat as well.

Casino promotions are often poorly strategized and poorly measured with no real understanding of their ROI. Did your promotion drive real revenue? Or were the customers already coming in anyway? Did they spend incremental gaming dollars because of your promotions or just shift their gaming budget to days where you threw a "promotional party" for them?

While the picture I may be painting of casino promotions excesses in North America may not be a pretty one, the good news is that if you can get your hands around your current promotional war chest and spend it in a customer focused way on those players who are eagerly spending their gaming dollars with you, there may be significant upside for you in your current promotional budget. Without spending a nickel more in marketing — a CFO's delight.

You're leaving millions on the (craps) table

There are some areas of gaming operations in which I don't claim expertise, but the craps table operation and experience is not one of them. I have dealt and supervised craps for many years in my career and, more meaningfully, I have played craps as my casino game of choice (in casinos around the world) when time and discretionary dollars allow it for over 30 years.

And if your casino offers craps, what I'm about to say will make you very uncomfortable. But I have come to the inescapable conclusion that, as an industry, we are leaving millions of dollars in craps profits on the table. And if you have craps, yes, that includes your casino, because I have yet to see one casino operator doing anything about it.

So you think I'm being too harsh? Well I'm going to share my staggering observations, and it will reduce to mere "chump change" what table game operators may be losing to theft, card counters or inefficient shuffling systems.

Yes, I've seen too much crap in craps. So here they are — my (free) multi-million dollar gifts to table game operators. Plug these holes and pursue these opportunities and your GM will be singing your praises (and wondering why he didn't think of this stuff):

The dice-setting epidemic — In craps, the players shoot the dice and whether they are superstitious or read a book on "overcoming the odds through dice control," I can tell you that the most players "set" the dice (with certain numbers being face up when they throw them), most of those players set the dice *really slow* and most casino operators do nothing about it. Solving this issue alone would contribute several million extra rolls (and decisions) per year to the worldwide table game industry. Now I am not suggesting that casinos summarily go out and roust their dice setters — hey we created this problem by allowing it and these are avid dice players, after all. But it does mean that you should be enforcing new procedures like having your stickman deliver the dice "pre-set" to the shooter, gradually begin establishing a reasonable time limit (a few seconds) in which a player must shoot the dice and start banning the very worst scofflaws from shooting the dice. And Shuffle Master or Progressive, here's some free consulting advice: start developing The Automatic Dice Shooter, it will be worth millions!

The novice string better — There is a whole species of them. They are not only novice craps players, but are also novice craps players who want to bet on *everything* on the table (usually $1 bets) and *hold up the entire craps game* to accomplish that ... *and we allow it!* OK, many of the bets these over eager novices are making are "sucker bets," but what they cost the house in lost dice rolls dwarfs their meager earning power. Train these avid new players so they earn you money and don't cost you money!

The "acorn" — When I dealt craps, I made a small fortune in tips in showing "acorns" how to play the game. An acorn is the rawest of novices, willing to listen to anything to learn the exciting game of craps. "Plant" an acorn right and he or she will grow into a "mighty oak" of a life-long craps player. Acorns are easy to spot — confused look, peering at the table and often will say things like, "How do you play this game?" I have seen literally thousands of acorns approach craps games, asking dealers how to play the game. The vast majority of the time, these acorns are brushed off, or given instruction that is incomplete, laced with dice jargon or is just plain confusing. Right now, our craps dealers are crushing acorns instead of planting them and it is costing us millions in lost immediate and long-term revenue opportunities.

Game pace — Depending on a variety of factors (number of craps players, types of bets being made, what numbers are rolled on the dice, supervisory control, dice dealer skill levels, etc.), every craps game has its own unique optimal game pace. And rarely does craps move at the right speed. Usually it moves too slow (costing money in lost decisions per hour) but sometimes it moves too fast (costing money in total bets made per hour). Sometimes a single dealer (usually the stickman) is the cause, moving too slow because they are bored or not motivated or too fast because they want to "run over" the craps players and kill the game.

Stupid procedures — There are dozens of these craps game rules and protocols that are currently costing us bazillions. Why does a craps game stop to take the count? Why are dice changed with each new shooter? Why are craps players not shown how to bet the "right amount" on certain bets, saving computing and payoff time? Why do operators buy cute, decorative dice layouts upon which dice won't slide but bounce all over the place? Why do stickpersons turn the dice, take them off certain combinations or purposefully bounce them off walls? Answer these questions and a million-dollar bonanza awaits.

I've been playing craps for decades. Our current games are slow, user unfriendly and inefficient and doing little to build long term dice business. I just thought you'd like to know. Yeah, thanks a million, Dennis.

A near-perfect casino promotion

I'm betting that you may have heard of a "National Customer Service Week" but have no idea when it is (it's in October). I'm also betting that your business almost certainly doesn't celebrate that week, even if you do care about your customers most weeks of the year. Well this is the story of a small locals casino that not only celebrates National Customer Service Week, but celebrates it *all month long*. And in doing so, it has come as close as I have seen to conducting the perfect casino promotion.

The Gold Dust West is a Reno locals casino. It is run by Black Hawk Gaming of Black Hawk, Colo., which also runs the Lodge and Gilpin Casinos in that market. There are no table games at the Gold Dust West, but the Wildwood restaurant offers food at a great value, the Gold Rush players club gives meaningful benefits that are actually easy to understand and the bartenders at the two video poker bars are among the best relationship builders in the casino biz. Yes, the Gold Dust West is a slot joint and, like most Nevada locals casinos, video poker predominates.

Gold Dust West is known for its "Cheers" atmosphere. So it is no surprise that it would choose to celebrate its customers with a whole Customer Service Month. But it is surprising how passionately, creatively and thoroughly Gold Dust West executes the whole thing, year after year.

This past October, Gold Dust West began its celebration of Customer Service Month with a direct-mail piece, alerting customers to the occasion once again and letting them know about all the neat ways Gold Dust West was going to honor them. There was free dessert all month in the Wildwood Restaurant. Club members received double cash back points on certain days in October, which became *all month long* if they filled out the guest survey included in the direct-mail offering and brought it in to the Gold Rush Players Club. There were "Worth A Million" drawings happening daily, weekly and monthly for amounts ranging from 10,000 cash points up to a million cash points, with guests earning entries by *voting for their favorite Gold Dust West employees throughout the month*. Employees were further honored by service shoppers who were anonymous customers at Gold Dust West during Customer Service Month, not looking for service snags and shortfalls, but scouring for Gold Dust's 40 best employees — to be honored with cash awards in a public recognition ceremony. And to promote it all, Gold Dust used its existing advertising budget and branded tag lines like: "Service. How The West Is One" and "You're Still The One" in its effective newspaper and TV spots. Many of the ads contained real employees that customers see every day.

So OK, you think Customer Service Month is pretty nifty, but what exactly makes it a "near-perfect" promotion? Well here's how I see it:

Unique opportunity — Gold Dust West has taken an existing and unappreciated occasion that speaks directly to the heart of its business — its *customers*.

Branding service — Using tags like: "Service. How The West Is One" is not a once-a-year splash, but a yearlong focus on how Gold Dust West values customer service.

Existing budget dollars — Gold Dust West does fairly extensive monthly advertising and promotions. So did they blow out the budget for this appreciation extravaganza? Not a bit. Pretty savvy, I think.

Gathering useful information — What better way to honor your guests than by asking for their honest opinions? During this month, Gold Dust West gathered this critical guest feedback but then also *made immediate changes and told their guests what they did*!

Employee involvement — A big, oversized promotional button stuck in an employee's uniform does not constitute "employee involvement" in a casino promotion. Gold Dust West used contests, "shopping for success" and employee-based advertising to not only stir interest, but also *active participation* in Customer Service Month.

Oh, I should mention, after this highly-effective Customer Service Month promotion was over, Gold Dust West followed up with a thank-you mailing in November to its customers. But not just any mailing — it invited customers to donate food to the annual Evelyn Mount Food Drive to receive an entry in the "World's Biggest Christmas Stocking" giveaway. Plus, there was an offer to, "use the Inn at Gold Dust West as your spare bedroom for friends and family" during the Thanksgiving holidays.

If you're going to have near-perfect casino promotions, you can't rest on your laurels. And Gold Dust West, in highly-instructive fashion, never does.

The greatest gaming innovations of all time

I have written and spoken about casino promotions for a long time. Every year in fact, I release a much-anticipated (or perhaps "little noticed") list of the Best (and Worst) Casino Promotions. The marketing efforts that make my annual list are pretty compelling, but they are also pretty diverse. I am as apt to recognize a casino that provides free oxygen refills for its seniors as I am to acknowledge a casino's million-dollar promotion.

But all of these years of evaluating, of casting marketing judgment, got me to pondering. In the long and storied history of gaming, what have been the quintessential marketing innovations, the unique developments and creations that have propelled the industry to new heights, the things without which our business wouldn't be the same?

Now this was a tough evaluation! I mean, how can you compare topless dance reviews with a $1.99 buffet? … Megabucks with a line pass? … double jackpots with free covered parking?

But recognize we must! (Consider it part of keeping the gaming history for future generations.) So here they are:

The greatest gaming innovations of all time:

The free (alcoholic) drink — I realize not all casinos allow themselves this great innovation — at least not the "free booze" variety — and that this tactic may seem predatory, but I don't care. Customers clamor for it and slurp it up in prodigious quantities and then spend more time and money at the casino because of it. "I spent $100 but at least I got a free drink." Marketing wizardry!

The megaresort — The building of the Mirage changed the face of gaming forever, so much so that many Las Vegas megaresorts now make more money at the "other" megaresort cash registers than they do at the gaming areas. And even local and regional casinos now routinely add megaresort elements to their facilities.

Penny slots — Thank the Aussies and Aristocrat for this one. What could be more powerful than a slot game with the cheapest cost possible, the ability to bet as much as at a dollar machine and a routinely great hold percentage?

Bill validators — When these came out, I didn't think anyone would use them (same thing with the credit meter instead of coins dropping). In fact, anything that allows faster play and more time in action is a strong innovation (ticket-in-ticket-out, credit button spins instead of handle pulls, etc.).

Single-deck blackjack — Some will disagree with me here (because of the vulnerability of single deck to the skilled player), but this game has had a hugely influential result on average blackjack players, making them feel "smart" about their game choice. That is why the new "6 to 5" single-deck game is so shortsighted.

The casino buffet — This includes both models, the "incredibly cheap but good, quality food" buffet and the "knock your eyeballs out, action cooking, around the world, higher-priced" version.

Player tracking/players clubs — Even though many casinos aren't real sophisticated yet in using these tools, most players are now trained to tether themselves to a slot machine with a bungee cord and other industries would kill for the quality of information we routinely receive.

Progressive jackpots — There is a certain fascination in watching prize pools grow (lottery slots, bingo, keno) and when this is both *rapid* and *achievable* (or, in the case of Megabucks, when it is *overdue*), progressive slot banks are flooded with dreamers.

Super Bowl parties — Not even the NFL getting its nose bent out of shape over "appropriate use of its telecasts" can stop this tidal wave of casinos combining food, drinks, parties, gambling and football.

Casino entertainers — I'm not referring to the mainstream headliners here — you know, the stars who could as easily play the Hollywood Bowl as the Caesars Palace showroom. No, I'm referring to those uniquely "casino" entertainers, who forever more will be linked to gaming — the Elvises, the Shecky Greenes, the Siegfried and Roys, the Danny Ganses, the Scintas, the George Carlins, even the Willie Nelsons.

Senior days — Not celebrated at every casino yet, but this is typically a "midweek day of value" for our beloved senior citizens, those wonderful drivers of our slot business, the folks with *both* the discretionary income and the time to pack their butts at our slot stools.

Wheel of Fortune — The standard for a branded slot game that continues to defy all notions of "average slot shelf life" and tap into that unique slot player psyche. Thousands of imitators and other branded at-tempts try to match its success, but none in its league. A true phenomenon.

The true "attraction" — Whether it's white tigers, or sharks, or a pirate show or even a 99-cent shrimp cocktail or a picture in front of a $1 million display, it's the uniquely casino marketing "flash" that draws hordes of people in the front doors.

And there you have it, my "lucky" list of 13 of the greatest gaming innovations of all time. In fact, let's add a 14th and we'll call it the "lucky charm." It's every rabbit's foot, every slot machine bell, every high-hit-frequency pay schedule on a slot machine — every *thing* casinos have done over time to make us feel that we will get lucky in their gambling joint. And that might be the strongest marketing innovation of all.

Little-known innovations

I have written often about many of the great innovations that have taken the gaming industry by storm in the last 15 to 20 years. Whether it's because gaming is a relatively new industry, or because there are so many competing needs in various aspects of our industry, (operations vs. regulation, marketing vs. finance, etc) or maybe because gaming just attracts some innovative, risk-taking types — whatever the reason, our industry is seemingly blessed with non-stop, big-time innovation and invention.

I mean, think about it. In a very short business history, the gaming industry has gone from having a very rudimentary system of qualifying customer-spending habits to sophisticated player-tracking systems and CRM technology. We've gone from having customers laboriously pump one coin at a time into our slot machines to a world of credit meters, virtual reels, ticket-in/ticket-out and bill validators. Our hotel operations are now likely to have yield management systems. Our security and surveillance areas routinely use digital technology and facial recognition software. Even our once-staid table game departments might have automatic shufflers, "no peek" devices and embedded chip technology.

Yes, the gaming industry has been, and continues to be, a hotbed of innovation and a model for continually finding new and better ways to run its basic business processes. In fact, we have been so good at innovation and development that I'm afraid we have not given some great, "little-known" innovations in gaming their due.

In fact, I'm betting there have been literally thousands of such small-time innovations that have made our employees' jobs easier, our customers' interactions with our organization more hassle-free or just more fun and our casinos just a bit more efficient and therefore more profitable.

I write about these from memory because, like many, I have no extensive list of these "two bit" innovations and probably missed noticing hundreds more because of their simplicity or subtlety. But it is important to recognize those that I do recall because taken collectively, their effect on our industry likely rivals that of any single earth-shattering gaming innovation of our time.

So here they are — some little-known innovations that make a difference:

208

The rounded shower curtain (Little Creek Hotel Casino, et. al.) — The concept was a simple one, if your hotel shower curtain is bowed out away from the tub (instead of parallel with the tub), your hotel guests — especially overweight ones — have more room and a better shower experience.

The GM's business card — When Coeur d'Alene Casino opened its new hotel, its CEO, Dave Matheson, just intuitively knew he wanted to have his business cards double as a free room offer for select guests. So he made the offer on the back of his cards. To this day, it is one of the few examples in our industry of "business cards that sell."

Executive "fun force" — In the early 1990s, Harrah's Las Vegas had a program where its senior managers spent four hours every month formally and positively impacting the experiences of its guests. They did things like serve champagne to guests waiting to check out at peak times, hand out chocolates in the slot areas and hang out with the table game funmeisters in the party pit. How strong is that???

Valet parking surprise — When Win-River Casino opened its brand new casino, it wanted to make a statement to its guests. At the new valet parking service, it washed every car's windshield and left a note (with a piece of candy) so that guests retrieving their car would know that Win-River said thanks and "wanted them to see their way safely home."

Cash back at the slots — Circus-Circus Reno wanted to understand the effect of slot cash back at its business and to see if it really mattered to slot players. Well before the advent of downloadable credits and kiosks, Circus-Circus deputized some frontline employees to redeem points for cash right at the machine, saving guests paperwork, hassle and time on device.

Art on room keys — On its hotel room keys, The Mill Casino depicted a work of art from a local (and talented) Native American artist. On the back of the room key it was mentioned that *prints were for sale in The Mill's gift shop*. How innovative!

Continuous innovations — When it comes to a never-ending *culture* of innovation, no one beats Barona Valley Ranch Resort & Casino. Imagine security officers posted on the driveway entrance at Barona and whose sole function is to wave to arriving and departing guests. Imagine dealers being certified as "Gamesmasters," being taught cheating techniques (so they could catch cheaters) and legitimate "soft hustling" techniques so they could make more tips. Imagine a "Sneak Preview Area" where slot players could try the absolute newest slot games … or a car-detailing service for VIPs … or having five times as many ATMs as a normal casino so guests don't have to wait in line. In fact, Barona teaches us all so well that a customer-focused cycle of small, continuous innovations can bring smiles to our guests' faces and make it much easier to do business with us.

And that is the power of innovation, no matter how small or seemingly insignificant.

Tributes

Barona! Eureka!

We have now worked with scores of tribal casinos in the nearly 10-year history of Raving. Our work usually involves interacting with the casino's marketing function and its marketing executives, but because of our approach (marketing is not a department, but should involve everyone in the tribal gaming enterprise!), we usually gain uncommon and valuable insight into each casino's entire DNA. We are honored to have become a trusted marketing resource in Indian Country and it is the work which brings us the most pride and sense of fulfillment.

While working with tribal casino clients, we are continually looking for the strengths upon which marketing progress can be made. Sometimes that strength is a great facility in a great location. Sometimes the strength is a GM or a marketing director who "gets it," who understands the importance of customer focus, or the integrated link between marketing and operations or how important it is to have motivated employees who bring their discretionary effort to their jobs. And every once in a while, that tribal casino's strength is its whole being — its entire way of doing business. And when we see it, we can only stand back and applaud (and of course point it out, so that other tribal gaming executives can learn from these industry leaders).

And we can find no better example of such an Indian gaming "marketing giant" than Barona Valley Ranch Resort & Casino.

We're betting that you've heard some of the "buzz" about Barona over the last few years and how it competes effectively with the other quality Indian gaming "mega-competitors" near San Diego, even though Barona easily has the worst location (and if you don't believe us, try driving up Wildcat Canyon Road to Barona any weekend evening!).

You may have heard about Barona's pioneering use of technology. It was the beta test site for the development of the high-powered Mariposa CRM software, which now sits squarely in IGT's bag of marketing tools. It pioneered TITO and it is currently pioneering server-based gaming. Barona has kiosks for its employees as well as its guests. It has mobile slot cashiers, a touch screen service monitor on its slots, biometrics (being used!), virtual promotions tumbler, a hotel key that serves as Barona's players club card and on and on and on. Barona clearly is a technology leader in Indian gaming. Heck, it is a technology leader in worldwide gaming!

If you haven't heard about Barona's pioneering use of technology, you may have heard about one of its dozens of marketing innovations. Barona has security officers waving to guests arriving by car and greeters at front doors welcoming guests (and aren't those nice personal touch points to counterbalance all that Barona technology?). Barona has a players-club-like program for its employees — the Ambassador Club. It has free auto detailing and towing service (don't get stuck on Wildcat Canyon Road!) for its VIPs. Seventy percent of Barona's coffee shop meals are served to active players on the casino floor. It has a new slot game "preview" area where players can always find the latest and greatest slots (not currently in California!). Yes, Barona knows innovation.

But what we are sure you don't know (because we haven't shared it until now), is our take on *why* Barona is such an exquisite example of the "whole marketing enchilada" and an Indian casino operating model that you should emulate, copy, steal from (legally of course) and aim toward. So here you have it:

Dennis and Toby's breakdown (no, not that kind of breakdown!) on the award-winning "brilliance of Barona":

Barona marries technology with "people" — Most casinos use technology to *reduce* the need for people, Barona uses it to *enable* its people to better touch its guests.

Barona knows its employees are critical to effective marketing — And it hires, pays, communicates to, rewards, empowers and motivates those employees as such.

Barona is not afraid to try new ideas — If it feels it will have a payoff, improve the guest (or employee) experience or potentially give it a competitive advantage, Barona will try it. Failure is both liberating and *essential*!

Barona likes to share its wisdom — Not only does Barona see the value in "leading the learning" for the gaming industry, it fully knows its competitors can't copy its "secret sauce" without the right chefs in the right restaurant with the right cooking process. You want to see how Barona does business? Just ask any of Barona's senior (even junior!) executives and they'll invite you down and probably comp your room!

The tribe and the management team are on the same page —
No offense to any other tribal gaming enterprises here, but the Barona Band of Mission Indians, its consultant, VCAT and its gaming management team are *really* in lockstep on what the gaming business really is and how they are all going to strategically execute it *together*.

Barona knows who its customers (really) are — And if you didn't know, they are the "Real Players," because Barona is the place "where the real players play." Not the casual player, not the lookie-loos, not the coupon hound, *the player*! And that is the clarity of focus that drives the whole Barona engine. *Hey, we are not for everybody* (just the most valuable players).

Don't think your Indian casino could ever get to be a Barona? Well, that's the best news of all. It wasn't too many years ago that Barona was in its first-generation sprung structure trying to figure out "who it wanted to be when it grew up." Well look at the beautiful Barona butterfly now, fluttering its wings in astonishing gaming marketing glory for all of Indian Country to marvel at and, hopefully, fly just as high as one day.

What can we do for Browne?

It's been awhile since I've penned a testimonial. It's not that there aren't any industry giants left to honor with my words and God knows the pool of "unsung casino heroes" out there is tremendously deep and largely unrecognized.

I guess I've just been remiss. But I aim to rectify that.

Now I know that in choosing to honor this particular person today, I'll be accused of being self-serving or, heaven forbid, even *wrong*.

I don't care. Even though this person is my friend, my confidante, my partner, my sounding board, my advisor and too often the brunt of my criticism, he is long past due my praise.

Steve Browne is the Customer Service Associate at Raving Consulting Company. Most people think he and I are partners or that he works for Raving, but he actually is an independent consultant who has created his own Customer Service Training business under the Raving brand. I couldn't be more proud of that division or more thankful for what Steve brings every day to the success of Raving.

It's hard to describe Steve Browne. He's a Texan who grew up rather well off, was a hippie for a short time at college in Colorado before becoming a ski bum in Lake Tahoe and, like many back then, falling into the gaming industry almost by accident.

Steve's gaming career is one of the more interesting stories in the business. As a fledgling table game junior manager in Lake Tahoe, he met a wealthy banker who wanted to buy a casino. In short order, with no money, no experience and no plan, Steve Browne was the general manager and part owner of a small locals casino in Carson City, Nev. called Cactus Jack's.

After a few years of bumbling and stumbling, Steve led Cactus Jack's to nine years of double-digit growth, with an incredibly simple and powerful strategy of "building meaningful, personal relationships with everyone who walked in the Cactus Jack's door." And then he sold his interest and "retired" from gaming for the first time to tend to his growing cigar bar business.

But enough of Steve's story. Let me share what I know of his soul.

Steve Browne now develops customer service programs and executes service training. He is a motivational speaker who inspires by connecting, by being relevant and by sharing his passion. I have seen him present now in front of several thousand casino employees, from the front line to the executive office, and I continue to be amazed at his impact. He still makes the hairs on my arms stand up when I listen to him.

Steve has no hearing in his right ear and watches his 17-year-old daughter, Katie, struggle daily with cerebral palsy. Somehow, I think, that has given him patience and perspective.

Steve Browne "grabs you" when you hear him speak or get cornered by him in a too-long and too-enjoyable conversation. Part of it, I believe, is his Texan B.S. and time-worn jokes, but more than that, Steve cares enough to make sure he connects, that he builds a relationship with you. He is never in a hurry when it comes to people.

Steve has been his own one-man crusade for the past 10 years. He speaks proudly and often emotionally about our industry as an "entertainment experience that enriches lives." He calls passionately for the recognition of those casino employees who give so much of themselves for our customers. Yes, Steve pioneered Bosses' Night at his casino, where the bosses would pull a shift in a frontline position to the delight of employees and customers alike. I love Steve Browne and consider him a great, true friend. Interestingly, he both inspires me and frustrates me, probably because I'm always in a hurry, and I don't have his patience or relationship-building skills.

What I have learned from Steve is how our casino business is truly about people. Yes we have games and lights and restaurants and hotels and spas ("all of that stuff," as Steve would say), but at the end of the day, what we sell is a connection between people. And while we think sometimes that our business is our slots and our rooms and our tables ('cause sure as hell we can count revenue there), it really is about Joe the valet parker and Javier the dealer and Flo the cage cashier. And whether he learned it or just always knew it, Steve Browne has been bringing the passion of his people message to our industry now for decades.

And whether you know Steve Browne or not, whether you care about his message or not, I'm hoping you can join me in thanking him — for making our casino lives a little brighter, our business mission a little clearer and our understanding and appreciation of people a little deeper.

And that's what Browne can do for you, or at least did for me.

Thanks, Phil

I first met Phil Satre some 20 years ago. I was the most junior of Harrah's Las Vegas managers and he was the chief operating officer of the entire company (called Promus at the time).

Having just assumed the role of table games instructor (called "Captain Casino" — and no, I'm not kidding), I was giving my 9:00 a.m. roulette lesson when I looked up from the layout to see our smiling COO watching my very hokey, but effective, dog-and-pony show on the joys of playing roulette.

Phil came up to me after the "How To Play Roulette" lesson, politely introduced himself (as if he needed to!) and complimented me on the quality of my table game instruction and the crowd it had attracted. Brownnoser that I was, I made a point to inform Phil that I was a fellow Stanford graduate and dropped the names of some of my fraternity brothers who had played on the Stanford football team with him. Ever gracious and interested, Phil was taking the time to connect with a very junior Harrah's supervisor in a very meaningful way. Over time, I found out that this relationship-building skill, whether with a dishwasher or a senior vice president, truly defined Phil Satre.

Within a few weeks of my button-popping first encounter with Phil, I received an inquiry from a representative of the Harrah's Northern Nevada properties in Reno and Lake Tahoe who had heard, no doubt from Phil, how great our Las Vegas table game instruction program was and asking if they could send down a Northern Nevada representative to learn how they could emulate our success and duplicate the instruction up north. Chalk up Phil Satre life lesson number two: see something of value and push the organization to expand that value.

Over the many years that have followed, as I have weaved my way through my own gaming career path, I have watched the meteoric rise of both Phil Satre and Harrah's Entertainment. And success couldn't have come to a nicer guy than Phil.

I think the true genius of Phil is somewhat lost in his style of deflecting praise and honors to others. That is why, while so many have seen the "best in breed" company that Harrah's has become, so few realize how much of that was directly because of Phil Satre.

Phil pushed Harrah's and the gaming industry to address problem gambling before most even knew what problem gambling was. He was studying the service profit chain and prodding Harrah's to be a great service company while others were investing in grand casino structural monuments. He was exploring branding and database marketing and "customer relationship management" before those now common and high-powered strategies had names.

Phil took management training and development at Harrah's to a new level by investing in his best people and looking for ways to find more "better people." He conceived the gaming industry's first program designed to give non-gaming senior executives a solid understanding of how the gaming business worked (The Harrah's Institute) so that Harrah's could broaden its executive talent pool and fuel gaming development projects.

He began a program named "Call Phil," where any Harrah's employee could talk to the Harrah's head honcho — confidentially — about absolutely anything at all, during a day that he had devoted to nothing but listening to his people. He performed his classic Elvis impersonation in front of his senior executive team. He took VIP customers on hunting trips. He had the foresight to hire Gary Loveman and saw *brilliance* when others saw only "an academic."

Phil Satre truly understood that the gaming business was not about making money (although Harrah's has made a lot of it), but was about creating *value* — for customers, employees and communities. He realized that happy employees made for happy customers and that loyal, happy customers provided business growth and competitive advantage. Managing to a balance sheet can never compete with managing to your customers — Phil knew that well.

The measure of a man can fairly be taken by what those around him say and how he leaves his mark on the world. Phil Satre has been universally loved and respected by all of those who have ever been part of his circle, and when he retired from the heady and hectic world of powerful gaming executives, he did so with class, with purpose and with the future of his company in good hands.

Phil Satre did not need to leave a generous scholarship fund for Harrah's employees, but he did. He did not need to so fervently build on the customer-focused legacy of Bill Harrah, but he did. And he certainly didn't need to take an interest in this fellow alum trying to make a sliver of Phil Satre's impact in the gaming industry, but he did.

Thanks, Phil, you made a real difference, for me and for the entire gaming industry.

For Steve Wood

You probably never met Steve Wood. His casino marketing career was a brief one. Steve died recently of cancer — at an all too young age — in his "retirement" city in Arizona.

Steve was the former CEO of one of those small, new-age California companies that seem to have sprouted up with regularity over the last three decades. He retired after this successful career as an industry leader to one of those warm, sunny areas in Arizona that people increasingly are retiring to.

Bored with not having anything to do for the first time in his life, Steve took a job to stay near one of the other passions in his life — golf. He became a ranger at a nearby country club. While he enjoyed that, as well as being able to play more golf than he had throughout his busy CEO tenure, he still felt something missing in his life.

One day, Steve saw an ad for a copy writer in the marketing department at the local tribal casino. Thinking that it sounded different and interesting, he applied for and got the job. And with his business background, it probably is no surprise that Steve soon became the casino's marketing director.

It was at this point in his life that I met Steve Wood. It was at a casino marketing seminar where, as a retired CEO, he had come to pick up a marketing background and a few "tricks of the trade." Steve Wood was not too proud to "go back to class" and in the few years that I knew him, he was not only always trying himself to continuously learn, but also encouraging his staff to do the same.

Steve was a kind, gentle and soft spoken man who was quick to laugh. I do not know anyone who knew him who did not like him — a rare thing in our often rough and tumble, fast paced gaming industry. Steve was truly one of the "good guys."

He took great pride in what he and his fledgling marketing team were able to accomplish at a small tribal casino, some 90 miles away from any major population base. He began to understand the "secrets" of marketing guru John Romero and when others in Steve's situation might have thrown gobs of money at advertising and big, fancy casino promotions, he was able to see the wisdom of having happy employees, strong relationships with the profitable regular customers and focused marketing efforts on the 20 percent of casino customers who drove 80 percent of the casino revenue.

Steve's reign as marketing director at this Arizona casino was a brief one, a very few years. You know how it goes: the GM who, likes and appreciates the marketing guy, moves on and the new GM brings in with him "his marketing person" who has been successful for him in the past. I guess you can't blame the new GM, but I have to believe he never took the time to know the heart, or the talent or the quality of Steve Wood.

Steve Wood died barely four months after the termination of his employment as the marketing director. I don't think those two things were related as cancer had severely ravaged his body in many places. And once the cancer was discovered, his ultimate treatment and suffering were brief. But maybe, just maybe, his marketing work and his extended casino family were part of what gave him life when he was so close to death.

I've had several people touch my life in a number of ways, but there has been no one other than Steve Wood who touched it so profoundly in such a short period of time. And I just know that there are many other people in the gaming industry who would say the same thing. And those lives he touched — with his genuineness, his gentleness and his caring — will long remain his living legacy. Steve Wood paid it forward.

Steve died in mid-November, while I was at the Global Gaming Expo. I received the news in a sad cell phone call from his wife. I was honored that, among his hundreds of friends, that she felt it important enough that Steve would have wanted her to alert me of his passing.

Three weeks prior to Steve Wood's death, I was preparing to take a small group of clients, associates and friends on our annual golf pilgrimage to Bandon, Ore. Steve had joined us the year before and he had a standing invitation to join us any year he could. Steve confirmed that he would be joining us again, but then called me back to say he was diagnosed with cancer but still thought he could make the trip after his first round of chemotherapy treatments. I realized that this golf trip, which he would never be able to make, was giving him reason to fight to get well. I held his spot for him and held his room at the hotel.

Less than a week before the golf trip, I talked to Steve on the phone. He'd been through chemo and also brain surgery to remove the cancer there. His words were slurred. He said he was "not quite in shape to golf." I told him that I would hold his room in case he felt well enough to travel and just wanted to come hang out with the guys. He said that was great and he would try. Two weeks later, he was gone.

Yes, Steve Wood might be merely a footnote in the annals of great casino marketing executives of the 21st century. But in two years he made a bigger impact on our industry than most of us will make in a lifetime. And in my mind, that makes him a casino marketing giant.

Goodbye Steve, I will deeply miss you.

A true casino marketer

I have met some very talented casino marketing executives in my 30-year gaming career. Certainly the dean of this marketing guru group is John Romero, and his common sense, results-oriented approach has been pointing the way to marketing wisdom for years (too bad more executives don't heed his advice).

Harrah's Entertainment, Inc. has a whole stable of marketing pros, most of whom come from outside the gaming industry. I have met other talented, knowledgeable marketing professionals at a number of large and small casinos across the country. They focus on the customer, they understand the integrated nature of the marketing process and they get results.

But the best casino marketer I know does not even have "marketing" in his title; he is a casino owner and operator. His casino properties are always market leaders and he spends more time on the floor of his casinos than some casinos' floor managers do.

His name is Jack Binion and if you don't know about his Horseshoe Casinos, then you don't know Jack.

I have never talked with Jack Binion, although I do seem to remember shaking his hand at some high falutin' gaming industry event. My wife did work for him when he ran the once-legendary Horseshoe in downtown Las Vegas and she remembers him fondly as someone who would stop to chat with her on a dead blackjack table. And as the Horseshoe was my favorite gaming haunt in the "old days" — 100X odds on the craps table and 50-cent Heinekens — I not only would see Jack Binion, but I would also glimpse the Horseshoe marketing magic.

Horseshoe Casinos (Mississippi, Louisiana and Illinois) have the most powerful marketing strategy in the gaming industry today and Jack Binion is the reason for it. Period!

Now I'm sure Jack would deflect this praise and give credit to his late father, Benny Binion, who crafted the original Horseshoe formula. But hey, I have seen second-generation gaming operators screw up their parents' success too! It takes a wise man to stick to a winning hand. Or as Benny Binion might have said, "Ya dance with who ya' brung."

Horseshoe Casinos are known for being places where "real gamblers" like to play. This "gambling joint" philosophy is extremely powerful and I'm frankly amazed that more casino properties haven't tried to emulate it. OK sure, there are some casinos that dabble in this "Best Place To Play" strategy (Cal-Neva in Reno, Copa Casino in Gulfport and maybe Barona Valley Ranch Resort & Casino near San Diego), but the Horseshoe Casinos own this positioning.

So what does Jack Binion know that other gaming operators don't, and why is he such a great marketer? Here's my take:

Jack knows what business we are in — While we all can now say "gaming entertainment" in unison, I'm sure Jack calls it "gambling," and he understands it's all about giving players a good gamble. While the corporate muckety-mucks use terms like "time on device" and "hit frequency" and "perception of winning," Jack continues to take all bets — large and small. I recall an old billboard of his in Las Vegas that said, "Best Odds. Highest Limits." Pretty strong stuff.

Jack knows the power of food — I know there are some casino operators that have quality food, but no one, I believe, uses food as a real marketing tool as well as Jack Binion. He eats in his own buffet and never cuts corners on quality. He understands the need for a first-class, but comfortable steakhouse to feed hungry table game players. When he realized he needed an Asian restaurant at his Tunica property, he bought out the franchise of the best Asian restaurant he knew and moved the entire operation (along with the chef) to Horseshoe Tunica.

And besides having great food, Jack has always been very liberal in feeding his gamblers, no matter if they had a players' club card or not. No matter what the "computer said."

Jack understands the value of employees and customer service — Although Horseshoe Gaming properties have service training, service shopping and other developed HR functions of the modern casino, the Horseshoe continues to take a simple, less-formal approach built on Benny Binion's old adage that, "You take care of your employees and they'll take care of your customers." Horseshoe pay and benefits are among the best in the industry, but the real power is likely in the visible senior management style where a frontline employee might be engaged on the floor by Jack Binion himself and the laid-back work environment where employees are left alone (in a good way) to take care of customers.

Jack knows his customers — And I don't mean their "demographic," or their "profile" or their "player history," but he knows them, personally. Oh sure, not every casino player, but certainly a great number of the best players, and I think that if Jack never even heard the phrase "Pareto Principle," I believe he understands the concept well. That explains why business nosedived at the Horseshoe in Las Vegas when Jack left. Jack took all of "his" players with him more effectively than any host with a black book of names ever could have dreamed of doing.

Jack Binion is not getting any younger and I wonder what will happen to his marketing philosophy, to his integrated, unique way of "how we do business around here." I worry that some corporation will buy his assets and then start a slow, painful process of cutting costs and lowering limits and bringing a faceless sameness to the Horseshoe Casinos. But what I really hope for is that there is some Jack Binion, Jr., or some poker-playing entrepreneur waiting in the wings who innately understands the marketing power of a good gamble, good grub and good old fashioned customer service.

Thanks, Jack, for showing us all how true casino marketing should be done, even if no one else dares to follow in your footsteps.

For Ginny

You probably don't know Ginny Shanks unless you are a gaming industry insider or a manager at Harrah's Entertainment, Inc. That's just the way she is.

Ginny recently retired from Harrah's as its senior vice president of brand management and was responsible for maximizing the value of Harrah's key strategic brands. She started at Harrah's Reno 25 years ago as the most junior of junior executives for Harrah's in-house advertising agency there. She obviously has broken the glass ceiling for women in the gaming industry and I don't believe anyone could hear the sound of the glass breaking when she did it.

Ginny and I were both junior marketing executives together at Harrah's Las Vegas 20 years ago. Our paths crossed often, even though I was a cub on the "casino" marketing side of the business and she was a fledgling on the "advertising" side.

The true measure of a friend is when you can remain friends and not see each other often. Ginny and I have remained friends for 20 years even though our career paths have swirled in different circles. But when we do see each other in a crowded airport, on a Southwest flight from Las Vegas to Reno (where we both live), for a few brief minutes at a casino marketing conference or at a too-seldom lunch at a local bistro, Ginny is always the same. She is glad to see me, funny, gracious and always tries to share candidly the reality of her world. I always feel that we are back in the employee dining room at Harrah's Las Vegas, kibitzing about how stupid some of our counterparts could be.

That's just the way she is.

As someone who likes to understand what makes programs or people successful, I have thought about how Ginny got to the top of her profession in an industry that, although (slowly) changing, is still very much an "Old Boys Club." Sure she is intelligent, witty and personable, but so are many women. OK, Harrah's is a progressive company that provided Ginny good training and an uncommon early culture of customer and employee focus, but that hardly can explain her trailblazing success (I still don't think that Harrah's today would be accused of having *too many* female senior executives). Some might say that the marketing side of the casino industry has had more opportunity for women. Maybe she was just lucky.

But for Ginny Shanks, I think the answers to explaining her success lie deeper and are instructive for all of us — not just women — in this wonderful and crazy business called gaming.

First of all, she is persistent. Some were reluctant to give her that first job at Harrah's Reno 25 years ago, but she knew she could do the job and she pushed until she had it. And sure, many women executives have had to persist, but not many have been able to do it with Ginny's style and class and grace.

That's just the way she is.

Ginny has never been afraid to speak bluntly to her superiors, who have usually been hard-headed, hard-charging men. I don't know if it is in her DNA, or it is an acquired skill or if she just realized that it is just good business to "shoot straight" no matter how big one's title is. But I have never seen Ginny speak other than what she considered to be the "business truth," not with fangs, but with finesse. I wonder who's giving Gary Loveman "the straight scoop" now that Ginny has retired from Harrah's.

Like most successful female executives, Ginny has had to juggle family with work, the boardroom with the back patio. I know this created many painful choices for her, but somehow she never sold her family or her company short.

That's just the way she is.

And while Ginny Shanks could have blazed her high-profile, senior-level career path all alone, she instead chose to do it with her friends — with Lynn, with Cameron, with Dennis. With countless associates that were not stepping stones, not obstacles, not relationships of convenience, but *people*. People whose life she was sure to enrich, whose day she never failed to fill with laughter, whose skills she unfailingly insisted on sharpening, for Ginny was both a mentor and a friend.

I'm not sure where Ginny's next career turn will take her. I'm sure she doesn't *have to* work, but she may *want to* take on a project, or a challenge or a new role where she can grow and learn and contribute to some team's success.

And perhaps if there is one defining virtue and lesson we can learn from this petite marketing giant of the gaming industry, it is that success is a team effort, that it should be shared, it should be open to men and women alike and that trying to leave a little of yourself with those you meet along the way, well it's a hell of a lot better way than just being a bureaucrat — even a successful one.

I think Ginny Shanks knows this. That's just the way she is.

Goodbye, old friend

The Horseshoe in downtown Las Vegas used to be my favorite gambling hangout. There was something about its aura.

The bars used to have 50-cent drinks and there was a $2 steak dinner in the downstairs restaurant. You could always find a 25-cent craps game and $1- and $2-blackjack tables were common.

But the Horseshoe was far from cheap.

It was well known that there were no limits at the Horseshoe's table games — or to be exact — *your limit was your first bet.* Somehow that just made the aura even a little better.

The Horseshoe wasn't a slot joint, but what slots it had, they were known to be loose as hell. It even had bingo for some time (until the local joints nibbled away at its local base) and, of course, the payoffs were the largest in town.

But perhaps it was the sports book and poker room that most gave the Horseshoe its flavor. Big limits and unbelievable characters hanging around. Somehow you just knew that *this* was a gambling joint.

The presence of Benny Binion only made the Horseshoe aura stronger. Even when he died, his spirit lived on there — almost magically — through his son, Jack.

I could tell you countless stories about the Horseshoe, for it was my favorite haunt for the 19 years that I lived in Las Vegas. The scores (and the dumps) at the craps tables ... the after-shift drinking bouts on 50-cent Heinekens ... the numerous shepherding trips of out-of-towners to have their free pictures taken in front of the Horseshoe's $1 million display, but more importantly, to see a *real* gambling joint.

No one at the Horseshoe used to ever ask me if I wanted to be rated. In fact that would have been the ultimate stupid question, for at the "Shoe" your play spoke for itself.

Customer service? Yeah, they paid you when you won and took your money when you lost. If you were hungry (and a gambler), they fed you. None of that modern textbook customer service from some college-bred training company.

Just a simple credo: Respect the gambler.

I was back at the Horseshoe a little while ago. I was eager and glad that some work had brought me to downtown Las Vegas. I wanted to revisit my old friend, to recapture those good old days at the Horse-shoe "gambling hall." Why it wasn't even called a "casino!!!"

Part of the aura.

I walked in from Fremont Street through the air curtain entrance. The old Big 6 wheel hadn't moved and still had a pretty girl dealing on it.

The craps tables were in the same place — ah, the memories began to stir.

Only there were fewer craps tables and more were closed than open. Even most of the open games had less than a full table of players.

Several of the craps dealers were not "experienced clerks," which is what you used to always find at the old Horseshoe. They might have snarled occasionally back then, but they could handle a packed craps game magnificently.

And then I noticed the sign: "$5,000 limit." Was I at the Horse-shoe??? Or had I stumbled into some downtown grind joint?

I played a little craps. But somehow it wasn't the same. Sure I lost a few hundred bucks, but at the old Horseshoe it would have felt like a battle scar. The aura would only have increased.

But now, I just felt empty … like I was at the funeral of some distant relative who I only vaguely knew.

I thought I'd get something to eat. But the downstairs restaurant was gone. The place where I'd eaten so many $2 steaks, the place where you could neutralize all those 50-cent Heinekens, the place where you could feel like a "winner" after dumping a few bucks or a few thousand? Gone, vanished.

I looked for comfort; familiar places. The cashier's cage was the same, the security chair next to it hadn't moved and an Asian gentleman was cashing out $12,000.

Good, a little relief.

But where was the poker room? Where were Puggy and Dolly and Johnny?

The room was not in its old, conspicuous space smack dab in the middle of the casino. All I could see left was part of the old mahogany railing that now framed some non-descript (and empty) slot space.

And what were those 5-cent video poker machines doing around my beloved craps tables? "No wonder no one is playing your craps games," I wanted to scream.

Certainly, there'd be refuge at an old, familiar, single-deck black-jack game.

I sat down. I bet $50. I lost. I bet $100. I lost. A floor person approached.

"Would you like to be rated?" he asked, not really caring.

That was enough. The aura was gone. "My" Horseshoe was gone. I rushed out to Fremont Street.

Goodbye, old friend.

My mentor

You don't see too many mentor relationships in the gaming industry. I'm not sure why that is. The business is a perfect environment to foster mentoring — lots of job functions and complexities, no organized career path structures, heavily built on relationships.

Perhaps it's because the casino industry has historically allowed career advancement through "juice," rather than skill and knowledge. Maybe it's because of all the focus on rules and regulations in the industry. Whatever the cause, gaming has typically lagged other industries in focusing on the "people" side of the business and career-development tools like mentoring.

But gaming *is* a very social business. Casino workers do play golf together, bowl together and (especially) drink together. I believe that whatever mentoring has existed in the gaming industry has sprung up from this informal network where casino employees socialize.

At least that's how I got to know my mentor, John O'Looney.

As I recall, the occasion was one of our property's golf tournaments and I was paired with John, who had recently come to our Las Vegas property as the vice president of casino operations with a reputation (made in Atlantic City) for being a hard charger who "made things happen." I was a little over a year removed from being a dealer and had just been "promoted" from my role as a gaming instructor to a temporary and experimental position called pit promotions and special events supervisor. My job was to come up with "stuff" to help drive table game business at our casino, certainly a difficult task as this was near the start of the slot revolution in the gaming industry and table games were beginning their slow decline.

I told John that I heard he liked "to do things" at the casino, meaning lots of programs, events and activities that would produce casino activity. Certainly it was a self-serving question, since at that time we did not even have a casino marketing department. And even though it wasn't much, the only one "doing things" was me.

"Well, I don't like to do things if they don't make sense," John answered my groveling. I had gotten my first lesson in a mentoring relationship that has lasted now for 15 years. And I'm still not sure why John O'Looney put me under his mentoring wing. Maybe he felt sorry for me. Maybe he just needed an eager, willing lackey to "make things happen."

So I became John's more-than-willing lackey and he became my mentor. He began to push me and prod me to try new things — major blackjack tournaments, VIP parties, an ESPN fight at our property, expanded junket business. Where we had been conducting one slot tournament a year, soon we were doing one a month. And I was the point person for all of it.

John O'Looney is an interesting guy, one I think you could certainly label as a "character." When I first met him he was driving a red Porsche and one of his first pieces of mentoring advice was, "if you want to spend more money, go out and make more money." Now there was an attractive alternative to my father's frugal preaching.

John never went to college, but still was one of the smartest gaming people that I knew. He liked to hang around on the casino floor and chitchat with the frontline employees, making friends and building relationships. At first this behavior seemed strange to me, until I realized that these employees soon were spilling their guts out to John and he got to know more about the gaming floor than any executive ensconced on the third floor behind a cherry wood desk.

My mentor made a point to keep the heat off me with upper management. In the free-spending world of casino marketing, it is easy to have your results questioned, even harpooned by the bean counters. John always told me not to worry about the budget battles or the marketing philosophy wars, but to just keep "making things happen."

The true measure of a mentor is how he or she shows appreciation to you. John pushed me to quick, significant raises, often beyond the maximum amount allowable. He gave me job titles with more stature. He exposed me to the little-known and heady world of company stock grants and options as bonuses for performance. He recommended me for the available company-wide awards and the recognition that went with them. He made available to me the company training and development programs for junior executives. He even encouraged me to look at job opportunities outside of our company because going on these interviews and talking about yourself in front of industry strangers was "good practice."

John O'Looney is now ensconced in a comfortable, underappreciated role with a major gaming company, not too many years from retirement. I still talk with him and occasionally socialize with him on a regular basis, at least as much as my hectic schedule will allow. I still receive and appreciate his frank opinions, his people-focused philosophy and his experienced words of advice. It is even better as, with time, this close mentor has become a close friend.

If you've never had a mentor, I encourage you to find one. If you've never been a mentor, then become one. If you're lucky, you'll find one, or be one, like John O'Looney. Thanks, John, for being *my* mentor and the kind of leader I can only hope to be.

Special Thanks

I have been blessed in my gaming career to work with — and become friends with — some of the finest people I can ever imagine knowing. Trying to thank all of them runs the risk of forgetting some of them. But I must try.

First of all, the current Raving team is the best group of people with whom I have ever worked. Christine Faria keeps every aspect of our business humming and is not afraid to get in my face when I am being stupid. Amy Hergenrother is the best salesperson and relationship builder I have ever seen. Toby O'Brien is an extraordinary friend whose misplaced trust in me hopefully has been miraculously validated. Kathy Ballew may be the youngest Raver, but there is a good chance that she is the wisest. Colleen Lenox has jumped into a Raving role that is as clear as mud and has done whatever it takes to be successful at it. Andy Holtmann may be very new, but he has babysat me for a long time.

Then there is the long list of people who are essentially responsible for everything I know in gaming and who have often ignored my hardheadedness in learning it. My mentor John O'Looney; the real casino marketing guru John Romero; research wizard and true "connector" Mike Meczka; "the smartest guy in gaming," Dr. Bill Eadington; ex-Harrah's CEO and fellow Stanford alum, Phil Satre — these people have unfailingly given me much more than I've given them. Anthony Curtis of Huntington Press has been a true friend and I thank him daily for *not* investing in Raving early on. David Kranes has shared his brilliance, his unique perspective and his friendship for years. Jean George carried me early in my career without a whimper, and until she realized how talented she was. Ginny Shanks hasn't changed in her journey from the cubicle to the boardroom and supported me with her wisdom and friendship for over 20 years.

Dave Zamarin, Dr. Data, has not only been an early mentor, but has continuously given me savvy feedback and advice every step of the way. Charles Anderer has ensured that one of my most positive partnerships has gone smoothly. T.J. Tejeda is a true Raver and a true friend. Andrew MacDonald has expertly juggled his role as client, friend and teacher with unparalleled ease. The late Riqui Leon and Dr. Peter Griffin taught me whatever it is I may know about casino tournaments and

234

casino math.

The list seems endless — Carol O'Hare, the late Shannon Bybee, Tom Jingoli, Ron Badouin, Joe Billhimer, the late Rex Buntain, Tom Brosig, Marty Williamson, Tom Bedell, Randy Carter, Melanie Dellas, Paul Doocey, Troy Simpson, Rick Lopez, Steve Karoul, Jerry Egelus, Angie Groeneveld, Rick Yuhas, Rudy McMillan, Jim Edelman, Jean Scott, Greg Shay, Tom Nugent, Howard Greenbaum, Scott Beeman, Deb Hilgeman, Ron Aller, Conrad Granito, Lynne Keller, Jon Lucas, Greg Liggett, Don Speer, Mike Moore, Tony Mavrides, the late Steve Wood, Barry Phillips, David McKee, Joe Malnerich, Sean McCreery, Dean McClain, Glenn Goulet, Aaron Rubin, Michael Peters, Max Rubin, Stuart Richey, Bruce Rowe, Joel Rovics, Yale Rowe, Scott Menke, Dave Schugar, Jimmy Wike, Todd Strusz, Jim Snead, Rob Salassi, Tim Taylor, John Thayer, Megan Taylor, Scott Voeller, Tom Walsh, Michael Weaver, Willy Allison, Larry Close, Deana Scott, Tom Guth, Hermann Pamminger, Frances Snyder, Jay Sevigny and Diana Bennett. I'm sorry to reduce all of you to a lengthy list, but your impact on my career was significant (and I'll see if I can get you an autographed book out of the deal).

And none of this would have happened without the support and understanding of my family — my wife Becky, son Casey, daughter Amy, aunt Mindy, cousin-more-like-my-brother Allen, my late mother and father Helen and Joe, sister Bev and brother in law Fran, niece and nephew Gretchen and Chris and every other relative who may have wondered, "what the hell I do," but made me feel I was good at it.

Finally, I thank my best friend, partner, golfing buddy, cigar connection and most motivating gaming guy I have ever seen, Steve Browne, for sharing his passion, his wisdom and his advice. This makes two books for me, Browne. Your turn!

About the Author

Dennis Conrad is the President and Chief Strategist of Raving Consulting Company, a marketing consulting company that in its 10 years of existence has worked with hundreds of casino companies and gaming vendors in North America, as well as several in Australia, Denmark, Austria, England, Italy, Slovenia, Puerto Rico, Panama, South Africa, Bulgaria and Peru. He has 35 years of gaming industry experience, in positions ranging from keno writer to corporate vice president.

Dennis is a graduate of Stanford University who played on the Stanford Golf Team with Tom Watson. He is also an avid gambler whose unique perspective as a casino customer, frontline casino employee, casino manager, corporate executive and gaming industry insider has made him one of the most effective and sought-after consultants in the gaming industry.

About Raving Consulting Company

Raving is the leading marketing consulting company in the gaming industry, having achieved its success by focusing on two simple principles: "Find out what your customers want and give it to them!" and "Whatever you need. The best you can get." Raving is an industry leader in conferences and seminars ("Best Speakers. Best Topics. Straight Talk."), customer service training (Steve Browne, Raving Service), access marketing for gaming vendors (Raving Partners) and marketing consulting services for casinos (Raving Casino Client Services).

If you are interested in the services of Raving, contact Amy Hergenrother, Vice President of Business Development at (775) 329-7864 or at amy@ravingconsulting.com. Or just drop Dennis a line at dennis@ravingconsulting.com.